Miranda Krestovnikoff's
BEST BRITISH
BEACHES

BEACH HUTS

FOR HIRE

INC:
2 DECKCHAIRS
2 WINDBREAKS
£10 a day

ALSO AVAILABLE:

WINDBREAKS
£2 per day

DECKCHAIRS
£2 per day

CALL NO 781350 699 TO BOOK
THE HUTS

contents

MAP REFERENCES

INTRODUCTION

The seas around our shores have created the most varied and beautiful coastline.

In the UK, no-one lives more than 75 miles away from the coast, and, I believe, we are all in some way connected with our shores. Our extraordinary coastline means that beaches have played an important part in many of our childhood memories and for those of us who don't live by the sea, the coast is a place that we can escape to, explore and discover.

I've done my fair share of exploring and discovering – some of my earliest childhood memories are of the beach at Deganwy, in Wales, where my grandmother lived: sometimes in the blazing sun and other times in the pouring rain, searching for sea shells, building sandcastles, burying my Dad in the sand, dodging seagulls – the usual stuff of seaside fun. Nowadays, I find the coast both exhilarating and relaxing – I relish a brisk and blustery cliff-top walk, a rainy day rock-pooling in my waterproofs or a rare snooze in the heat of the midday sun. Our beaches offer all of these things, and more, and that's what makes them so special and unique.

Being an island nation, we have, perhaps, a different attitude towards our beaches than other Europeans. Come holiday-time, we don't have the Alps to escape to, or vast inland lakes – and, therefore, we have built up a relationship with our beaches in all their different forms. This love affair exploded during the Industrial Revolution when the railways suddenly made our coastline more accessible to people further inland. The age of the package holiday had begun and we all headed for the coast. St. Ives, Cromer, Whitby and Blackpool all became holiday hotspots – miles of sandy beach to lounge around on and play in. There are those of us who long to find a quiet secluded spot to sit, read and think; others, maybe with family, who seek the hustle and bustle of the classic bucket-and-spade beach with ice creams for the children and donkey rides. You may want an energetic walk with a stunning view or just to seek the wilder side of the coastline: watching waders at sunrise or puffins at sunset. I hope that there is something for you here.

We may instantly think of a beach in a romantic way with long miles of sand like the great expanse at Bournemouth, but sometimes forget that a beach can also be shingle, pebbly or rocky – just think of the 18 miles of pebbles at Chesil Beach! And what is on offer when you get there varies enormously, thanks to our geology and ancient history. Beaches, like people, come in many shapes and forms – each one is individual with its own character and personality. Sometimes the craggy ones that are more challenging turn out to be the ones with the most to offer!

In *Best British Beaches*, I wanted to review more than 100 of our best beaches. I have chosen many for personal reasons, others are simply timeless classics or are listed here because of their outstanding credentials. Some have been selected for excellent beachcombing, wildlife, bird watching and fossils while others have been chosen purely for their wonderful white sands and crystal clear waters. It is impossible to be comprehensive – everyone has their own favourites – but hopefully this book will encourage you to make some new discoveries and to nurture this great British love affair with the seaside, both for yourselves and for the next generation.

south west

South-west England is Britain's most popular holiday destination, with a long and varied coastline that encompasses the flat lands of Somerset, the high moors of Devon, the rocky coves of Cornwall, the dramatic chalk cliffs and rock formations of Dorset – and the Isles of Scilly and Channel Islands. You can experience the superb and varied coastal scenery on the 630 mile (1,014km) South West Coast Path, which leads all the way from Minehead in Somerset to Poole in Dorset.

The north and west shores from Ilfracombe to Land's End are battered by Atlantic winds and waves – they can reach 50ft (15m) in the seas beyond the Isles of Scilly – caused by severe storms as far away as Cape Horn. The cliffs are indented by tiny, rocky coves and long, sandy bays, for example at Woolacombe Sands and St. Ives Bay; or eroded into dramatic shapes as at Bedruthan Steps. This is the best surfing coast, with the beaches around Newquay and Sennen Cove being especially highly rated.

LANDS END

NEW YORK 3147   JOHN O'GROATS 874

ISLES OF SCILLY 28
LONGSHIPS LIGHTHOUSE 1½

ISLES OF SCILLY

Bryher •
• Pentle Bay

• The Bar and Cove Vean

Woolacombe Sands •
• Saunton Sand
Westward Ho! •

DEV

Constantine Bay •
• Bedruthan Steps

CORNWALL

Bigbury on Sea • •
Thurlestone
Sands

• St. Ives Bay
• Sennen Cove
• Praa Sands
• Porthcurno
Kynance Cove • • Kennack Sands

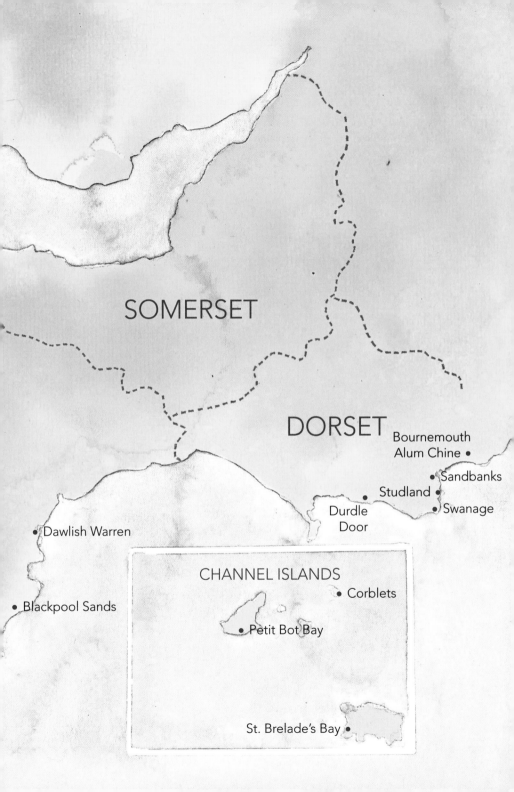

SOMERSET

DORSET Bournemouth
Alum Chine •
• Sandbanks
Studland •
Durdle • Swanage
Door

• Dawlish Warren

CHANNEL ISLANDS
• Corblets

• Blackpool Sands

• Petit Bot Bay

St. Brelade's Bay •

Constantine Bay

NEAREST TOWN PADSTOW

Constantine Bay was famously Margaret Thatcher's favourite British beach destination when she was prime minister in the 1980s. It's a crescent-shaped bay, contained by low headlands, with a deep, sandy beach, backed by massive marram-grass dunes and the Trevose golf and country club. It's a remote spot – although only a few miles away from the thriving fishing town of Padstow. Access is by single-track roads that get extremely congested in the height of summer (there is very little parking near the beach, and people often prefer to leave their cars in Treyarnon and walk the 10 minutes to Constantine Bay).

There is a rocky reef, which is good for snorkelling in calm weather. The bay is also a very popular surfing beach, with left and right waves, although it has difficult rip currents and is not recommended for beginners. Swimmers should take care, too, as there are many rocks in the bay.

Just north beyond Constantine Bay, and accessible by wooden steps at high tide, is Booby's Bay, a smaller, sandy beach with rocky outcrops. From here, the South West Coast Path leads to a sea cave at Round Hole and to the cliffs around Trevose Head, where you might catch sight of grey seals (pictured right) or dolphins, as well as purple sandpipers, corn and Lapland buntings during migration seasons.

INFORMATION

Beach Type	Sand
Facilities	Toilets (with disabled facilities)
Activities	This is a popular surf spot, however, it is advised that it is only suitable for experienced surfers due to the unpredictability of the waves
Parking	Limited parking available on the beach (approximately 30 spaces), further parking is available ½ mile up the road
Information	Padstow Tourist Information Centre (01841 533449)
Lifeguard Cover	May to September
Dogs	Welcome, but must be kept on a lead at all times
Useful Websites	www.ncdc.gov.uk www.visitcornwall.com

Bedruthan Steps

NEAREST TOWN NEWQUAY

Standing on the rugged cliffs above Bedruthan Steps, you're face to face with one of Cornwall's wildest and most breathtaking views, with towering rock stacks shaped like turrets, sphinxes and ice-cream whirls splayed across the beach below. Legend has it that Bedruthan, a Cornish giant, scattered the stacks from Pendarves Island to Diggory's Island as stepping stones over the bay. At high tide, the craggy outcrops are surrounded by raging seas, but when the tide retreats a mile-long stretch of flat sand is revealed around the rocky monoliths.

If you're feeling fit and brave, take the steps down to the beach from the National Trust Carnewas car park – although the descent is steep, often slippery and dangerous, with wire netting bolted into the cliff face to stop rock falls, it's well worth making the effort.

You can wander around the stacks themselves; up close they're encrusted with barnacles and extensive colonies of mussels. There's Queen Bess Rock, which used to have the profile, ruff and farthingale of Queen Elizabeth I, until, in 1980, the seas claimed her headdress – now it looks more like a whirled pyramid. Samaritan Rock got its name from the *Samaritan* ship that was wrecked here in 1846, spilling its cargo of barrelled beef and cloth onto the shores – the locals who salvaged the booty nicknamed the stack the 'Good Samaritan'. Sometimes the sands shift and, when they do, it's said that you can see the ship's bones and keel at the base of the rock.

Walk beyond the stacks, through a narrow channel past an eroded sea arch, and you come out on a clear, small beach beyond – it's a good place for sunbathing, but it's unsafe to swim or surf anywhere on Bedruthan Steps as the undercurrents are treacherous. Watch the time too, as the tides comes in fast and can trap the unwary on the rocks. Once you've made your way back up the precipitous steps to the cliff top above there are two choices. Head for a fresh mackerel sandwich and cream tea in the lovely tearoom overlooking the beach (there are also toilets and a National Trust shop in Carnewas car park). Or set off along the stunning South West Coast Path to visit the Iron Age fort of Redcliff Castle nearby, and have the chance to see petrels, shags, fulmar and razorbills nesting along the cliffs.

Beach Type	Sand
Facilities	Toilets available in the car park, tea room and garden (National Trust concession) in Carnewas car park overlooking the coast
Activities	None and swimming is not advised
Parking	Pay parking available – seasonal charge
Information	Bedruthan Steps is closed from November to February because of the increased likelihood of rock falls during the winter weather. Carnewas National Trust (01637 860563)
Lifeguard Cover	None
Dogs	Welcome all year
Useful Websites	www.cornwallbeachguide.co.uk www.nationaltrust.org.uk

St. Ives Bay

NEAREST TOWN ST. IVES

St. Ives has been Cornwall's artistic hub for more than 100 years. Painters and sculptors have been attracted by its quaint cobbled streets, granite fisherman's cottages, busy fishing harbour and idyllic natural setting on a rocky isthmus, surrounded by sea on three sides. There are three beaches in St. Ives, each with a different ambience. Firstly, the magnificent surfing beach at Porthmeor, overlooked by the Tate St. Ives art gallery, is pummelled by Atlantic rollers and winds. Secondly, Porthgwidden beach (pictured) is a small, sandy treasure, with sheltered swimming and a good café. Thirdly, Porthminster beach, stretching half a mile from town, is a traditional family destination, sheltered and calm, with beach huts, a putting green, and the restaurant with the best views (and food) in town, the renowned Porthminster Beach Café.

The town stands at the head of north Cornwall's largest bay, which has miles of golden sand, stretching around to Godrevy Point and the lighthouse (made famous in Virginia Woolf's book, *To The Lighthouse*). You can walk on the South West Coast Path from Porthminster beach along the cliffs and wooded headland to neighbouring Carbis Bay and mile-wide Porth Kidney sands (at low tide). On the other side of the River Hayle (the tidal estuary is unsafe for bathing) you come to Hayle Towans, a 3 mile (5km) stretch of beach that includes the smaller beaches of Mexico Towans, Upton Towans and Gwythian Towans, all of which offer good swimming and watersports – although the surfing is better towards Gwythian at the eastern end of the bay.

Beach Type	Sandy
Facilities	Toilets (including disabled facilities), a variety of cafés, restaurants and shops are available in the area. Lost child centre, first aid post and a slipway
Activities	There are so many things to do in the area, we just haven't got the space to list them all – see Useful Websites for further information and events listings
Parking	Pay parking available
Information	St. Ives Tourist Information Centre (01736 796297)
Lifeguard Cover	June to September
Dogs	Restrictions from Easter to September
Useful Websites	www.stives-cornwall.co.uk www.cornwallbeachguide.co.uk

Sennen Cove
NEAREST TOWN SENNEN

Sennen Cove is just a mile north of Land's End, the most westerly point of mainland England. Despite the name, it's more of a bay than a cove, stretching from the rocky headland of Pedn-men-Du along Whitesand Bay to the vertical sea cliffs of Aire Point. It's an idyllic, romantic spot, with white, marram dune-backed sands, deep turquoise sea and spectacular sunsets over to the Isles of Scilly just 28 miles (45km) away. In Arthurian legend, the sunken kingdom of Lyonesse was thought to stretch from here to the Isles of Scilly.

At the Sennen Cove end of the bay, there's a small harbour arm, with two slipways and an RNLI lifeboat station. Behind are a few stone cottages, a terraced beach restaurant (with good views of the bay and the sunsets), the 17th-century Old Success Inn, and a Roundhouse and Capstan Gallery, once used to winch boats from the shore. It's a picturesque spot.

Today, the west-facing beach is extremely popular with surfers: the bigger swell and winds are usually found at the Gwenvor end of the beach towards Aire Point, but beware of rip currents. The walk along the rocky cliffs on the South West Coastal Path to Land's End (there is also a cycleway) is well worth it: you're likely to catch sight of unusual wildlife including purple sandpipers, redshanks, winged plovers, wheatear and whimbrel, depending on the season. Dolphins often frolic in the bay, and you can hire horses to ride along the cliffs above for the most breathtaking views of the shoreline and seas beyond.

INFORMATION	**Beach Type**	Sand
	Facilities	Toilets (with disabled facilities) and showers, restaurants, cafés and a beach shop, first aid post and pier
	Activities	Surf tuition available (Smart Surf: 01736 871817 or Sennen Surfing Centre: 01736 871561)
	Parking	Pay parking available
	Information	Penzance Tourist Information Centre (01736 362207)
	Lifeguard Cover	May to September
	Dogs	Restrictions apply from May to September
	Useful Websites	www.visit-westcornwall.com www.sennen-cove.com

INFORMATION

Beach Type	Sand
Facilities	Toilets (with disabled facilities), café and a lifeguard hut
Activities	The Porthcurno Telegraph Museum (01736 810966) is approximately a 10 minute walk from the beach
Parking	Pay parking available
Information	Penzance Tourist Information Centre (01736 362207)
Lifeguard Cover	May until September
Dogs	Not permitted
Useful Websites	www.visit-westcornwall.com www.cornwallbeachguide.co.uk

Porthcurno

NEAREST TOWN PENZANCE

Just 3 miles (5km) along the South West Coast Path from Land's End, the scenery is astounding: vertiginous 230ft (70m) high cliffs drop down to small, sandy coves at Porthcurno and neighbouring Green Bay, a tidal beach accessible from Porthcurno beach at low tide. The shores are washed by aquamarine seas; there's a peninsula with a huge granite rocking stone called Logan Rock, precariously balanced in the middle (in 1824, as a drunken prank it was pushed over the cliff – there was a huge public outcry and it took 60 men seven months to restore it to its original position). The tour de force is the Minack Theatre, an open-air, Greek-inspired amphitheatre built high into the rocks on the cliffs overlooking the bay. From May to September, you can watch plays and music being performed here against the stunning backdrop of Porthcurno Bay and the Logan Rock headland beyond.

Despite its situation, access to Porthcurno Bay is easy by road: there's a car park 220yd (200m) away, and a wide footpath leads down to the beach. From the late 19th century, Porthcurno was Britain's most important cable and communications station, with underwater cables stretching as far as India. The underground Porthcurno Telegraph Museum near the beach is well worth a visit.

Praa Sands

NEAREST TOWN HELSTON

Praa (pronounced 'pray') Sands is a mile-long sandy, dune-backed beach facing south into Mount's Bay and stretching between the headlands of Hoe Point and Rinsey Head. It's a popular surfing beach, with powerful waves, and gets very busy in summer – there are cafés, bars and a surf shop in the village just off the beach. In the sand dunes and grasses there is a wide range of wildlife – you might see badgers and rabbits, and wild flowers such as bright yellow lady's bedstraw, wild thyme and eyebright.

Praa Sands is perhaps best known for its interesting geology: at the back of the beach, near the dunes, there is a dark area that is a Quaternary Age peat bed overlaying a silt of cobbles and gravel. Towards Rinsey Head, you can also see light-coloured granite sheets and veins in the rocks, formed when molten magma was pushed up from the earth's mantle into country rocks, then rapidly cooled. Just inland is Pengersick Castle, a 16th-century castellated tower that is reputed to be haunted by a busy conglomerate of ghosts: an ethereal lady, a black dog, a black-robed monk and a sailor who wanders around the gardens. The castle is private, but open to visitors on request.

Beach Type	Sand
Facilities	Toilets (with disabled facilities), first aid post, lost child centre, shops, campsite and a caravan park, café, restaurant, pub and a slipway
Activities	Surf tuition available (Sennen Surfing Centre: 01736 871561)
Parking	Two pay car parks available
Information	Kerrier Council (01209 614000)
Lifeguard Cover	Easter holiday – full cover, then weekends until 1st May. Full cover resumes from 1st May to 30th September, then weekends only until the October half term. Full cover during the half term holidays
Dogs	Restrictions apply from Easter to October
Useful Websites	www.cornwallbeachguide.co.uk www.kerrier.gov.uk

INFORMATION

Beach Type	Sand
Facilities	Toilets (with baby changing facilities) in the car park and Kynance Cove Café (01326 290436)
Activities	No organised activities
Parking	Pay parking available
Information	National Trust South West Cornwall Office (01326 561407)
Lifeguard Cover	None
Dogs	Not permitted between Easter and October.
Useful Websites	www.cornwallbeachguide.co.uk www.visitcornwall.com www.nationaltrust.org.uk

Kynance Cove

NEAREST TOWN LIZARD

The stunning, aquamarine waters and white sands of Kynance Cove are just 2 miles (3km) from the Lizard, the most southerly tip of mainland England. Grass-topped cliffs sweep down to the sea from where there are dramatic views of the rocky outcrops and stacks – Devil's Bellows, Steeple Rock, Asparagus Island (with the sucking cave crack called the Devil's Postbox) and Man O War Rock – eroded from the cliffs. At low tide three small sandy bays are accessible, and you can explore the Ladies' Bathing Pool, the Parlour and the Drawing Room – fascinating caves cut deep into the rocks and named when Kynance Cove was a popular holiday destination in Victorian times.

In the cliffs and on the beach you'll find red and green serpentine stones (so-called because of their snakeskin markings) for which the Lizard is renowned. The cliff walks north and south are spectacular, and the geology and microclimate make for interesting flora – you might see wild plants such as lady's bedstraw, bloody cranesbill, milkwort, the rare Cornish heath, self-heal, and the cerise and yellow flowers of the hottentot fig (pictured right). The Lizard is looked after by the National Trust, and there is an excellent NT eco café in the cove, with a turf roof and wool insulation. The black huts of nearby Lizard Wireless Station, where Marconi pioneered his wireless telegraph, is also worth a visit.

Kennack Sands

NEAREST TOWN HELSTON

This unusual silver sand and shingle beach, on the eastern side of the Lizard, is divided by Carn Kennack hill and Caervarrack shore rocks into two distinct beach areas at high tide. The bigger, western beach is sandy (with a café, car park and toilets), and is well known as a safe swimming and surfing spot, with 5ft- (1.5m) waves in good conditions.

At high tides, you can approach the eastern beach by footpath over Carn Kennack. It's a nature reserve, and the Lizard's unusual calcium-rich soil means that many rare species grow in the dunes and grasses here – look out for galingale, fringed rupturewort, lesser meadow rue and suffocated clover. The eastern beach is quieter and rockier, and beachcombers can find green and pink serpentine pebbles and, perhaps, rare black hetaerolite. It's also a good angling spot for bass and flatfish.

There are interesting walks along the South West Coast Path to the Mesolithic and Iron Age hill settlements at Poldowrian and Carrick Luz to the east, and to Carleon Cove and the remains of a once-thriving pilchard fishery, to the west.

INFORMATION

Beach Type	Sand
Facilities	Toilets, café/shop and a slipway
Activities	No organised activities
Parking	Pay parking available
Information	Lizard Natural Nature Reserve (01326 240808)
Lifeguard Cover	May to September
Dogs	Banned on the west beach from Easter to October. Welcome on the east beach all year
Useful Websites	www.cornwallbeachguide.co.uk www.visitcornwall.com

Bigbury on Sea
NEAREST TOWN BIGBURY

Bigbury on Sea is set in the South Devon Area of Outstanding Natural Beauty in the estuary of the River Avon. The town slopes down to the wide, golden sands of the beach, with spectacular views of Burgh Island and the imposing Art Deco Burgh Island Hotel just 220yd (200m) out to sea. You can walk over the sands to the private island at low tides or take the sea tractor at high tides (pictured far right) – a unique raised carriage on huge hydraulic tractor wheels, designed in 1969 in exchange for a case of champagne. The stylish hotel was a haunt of Noel Coward and Agatha Christie in the 1930s and the island's setting inspired her novel *And Then There Were None*. You can wander around the island to see the World War II pill boxes and observation post, perhaps even the ghost of notorious smuggler Tom Crocker still looking for his lost treasure, and enjoy a plate of oysters in the 14th-century Pilchard Inn.

The beach is a perfect spot for a family day out, with safe swimming (away from the river) on the gently shelving sands. Canoeing and windsurfing are popular and, when the tide is out, you often seen kite-buggies swinging around the sands of the bay.

Beach Type		Sand
Facilities		Toilets (with disabled facilities), first aid, shower facilities, a slipway and disabled access to the beach. Refreshments kiosks available during the summer. Cafés and beach shops close by in the local village
Activities		Visit Burgh Island by seatractor (www.burghisland.com/seatractor.html) or on foot if the tide is right
Parking Information		Pay parking (with disabled access) Modbury Tourist Information Centre (01548 830159)
Lifeguard Cover		May to September
Dogs		Restrictions apply May to September
Useful Websites		www.devonlink.co.uk www.burghisland.com

Thurlestone Sands

NEAREST TOWN THURLESTONE

Thurlestone is a picture-postcard pretty Devon village, with thatched cottages, rambling flower gardens, a 13th-century church and a 16th-century inn that was built with timbers from the sunken Spanish Armada ship *San Pedro El Major*, which was wrecked off the coast. The beach itself is wide and sandy, with rocky outcrops stretching out at low tide to Thurlestone Rock, a dramatic sea arch made of new red sandstone, once painted by J.M.W Turner. The rock pools are full of crabs, mussels, unusual seaweeds and other marine life.

Thurlestone Sands is a favourite spot for watersports including kayaking, windsurfing and diving – visibility is good in the clear water and there are more than 30 wrecks in the area, some of which can be explored. Swimming is safe too. There are spectacular walks along the sea cliffs of the South West Coast Path to Hope Cove and harbour, or west past the Thurlestone golf course and Loam Castle, where Roman remains have been found. Look out for unusual wild flowers and birds – you'll see stonechats, wheatears and fulmars and perhaps even rare birds such as garganey ducks and least sandpipers, which have been spotted here.

INFORMATION

Beach Type	Sand and fine shingle
Facilities	Toilets, kiosk and shop nearby
Activities	Windsurfing, kayaking and diving are popular activities. There are also scuba diving excursions (01865 311448) available
Parking	Pay parking available
Information	Kingsbridge Tourist Information Centre (01548 853195) or Southam District Council
Lifeguard Cover	May to September
Dogs	Welcome all year
Useful Websites	www.thurlestonebeach.co.uk www.southams.gov.uk

Beach Type	Sand
Facilities	Toilets (with disabled facilities and baby changing), outside showers, beach shop, café/restaurant, deck chairs and windbreaks are available for hire
Activities	A variety of watersports available (Lushwind Watersports: 07849 758987). A bathing raft during the summer and sand boxes for children. Blackpool Gardens (01803 770606) is nearby
Parking	Pay parking during the summer and weekends, free parking in the winter
Information	Dartmouth Tourist Information Centre (01803 834224)
Lifeguard Cover	July to September
Dogs	Not permitted
Useful Websites	www.blackpoolsands.co.uk

Blackpool Sands

NEAREST TOWN DARTMOUTH

This is one of the most picturesque, perfectly formed beaches in the country: a crescent, two-thirds of a mile long, with coarse, golden sand and aquamarine seas, backed by the emerald green of steeply wooded cliffs in the beautiful South Hams. Facing south east, its (usually) calm, sheltered waters make it a popular summer destination, and it has everything you need for a great beach day out, including a sandcastle building pit for little ones, an eco-café, shop, award-winning toilets and watersports equipment for hire. Try sailing, windsurfing, body-boarding, canoeing and even offshore swimming – the sands shelve away sharply and there is a floating raft with a ladder in the sea that you can venture out to during the summer (plus lifeguards just in case).

Blackpool Gardens, a restored 19th-century sub-tropical garden, with collections of palms, cork trees and ferns, is accessed through an entrance in the car park, and has spectacular views overlooking the bay. There are strenuous walks along the South West Coast Path on the cliffs and jungly woodlands behind, and there's a small but fascinating marine museum with a collection of ships-in-bottles in a 17th-century merchant's house in nearby Dartmouth, which is well worth the trip.

INFORMATION

Beach Type	Sand and shingle
Facilities	Toilets (with disabled facilities), shower facilities, café/restaurants, first aid post, slipway, camp sites and caravan parks locally, beach hut, wheelchair and deck chair hire available.
Activities	Amusements and a summer entertainment programme between July and August
Parking	Pay parking (including disabled access) available
Information	Teignmouth Tourist Information Centre (01626 215665)
Lifeguard Cover	May to September
Dogs	Not permitted between groyne 9 and Warren Point from May to September
Useful Websites	www.dawlishwarren.com

Dawlish Warren

NEAREST TOWN DAWLISH

Dawlish Warren is a sand spit about 1¼ miles (2km) long by 220yd (500m) wide, on the west side of Lyme Bay jutting across the wide estuary mouth of the River Exe almost to Exmouth. It's a stunning location, with clear blue seas on three sides and a wide beach, which at low tides connects to a large sandbank called Pole Sand. The beach stretches down from Warren Point to Langstone Rock, an extraordinary landmark of new red sandstone standing 49ft (15m) high.

Dawlish Warren is a popular spot: the beach has been awarded a Blue Flag for ten consecutive years and at the neck of the spit lies the Warren holiday village, with amusement arcades, karting, children's rides and cafes – around 850,000 people are said to visit the area each year.

The spit has probably been in existence since at least the 16th century and is now a National Nature Reserve. It's constantly changing, being eroded by longshore drift, estuarine tides and rising sea levels. Today it is protected partly by a concrete sea wall, boulders and groynes. There are varied habitats on the spit including salt marshes, dunes, ponds and reedbeds, as well as a hummocky golf course in the inner warren. The outer warren is open to visitors and is a haven for wildlife, with more than 450 plant species including the rare sand crocus (pictured right) and petalwort, and many unusual birds, insects and fungi.

Westward Ho!

NEAREST TOWN BIDEFORD

Westward Ho! has two claims to fame: it's the only placename in Britain with an exclamation mark, and it's the only British town named after a book, Charles Kingsley's popular 1855 novel *Westward Ho!* (a seafaring yarn that he wrote in nearby Bideford). Before the 1860s, the coastline here consisted of a pebble ridge, with a 2 mile (3km) stretch of sand at low tide. The Victorians built the resort at high speed to exploit the popularity of Kingsley's book, and Westward Ho! has since become one of Devon's most popular family beaches, with various holiday camps in the vicinity. Along the promenade there is a row of eye-catching traditional beach huts, plus cafés, amusement arcades, a putting green, deck chair hire and many other facilities including watersports.

At very low tides you can see the remnants of a Mesolithic sunken forest and peat beds – sea levels have altered dramatically in this area (in the cliffs you can see evidence that the sea was once 26ft (8m) higher) and the coastline is constantly changing. The pebble ridge extends north and behind it, jutting out into the Taw/Torridge estuary, lie the dunes, periglacial sediments and marsh beds of Northam Burrows Country Park, a good spot for wildlife and bird-watching.

INFORMATION

Beach Type	Sand backing onto a pebble ridge
Facilities	Toilets (with disabled facilities and baby changing), café/restaurant, first aid, lost child centre, promenade, camp site, deck chair hire and a slipway
Activities	Amusement arcades, kitesports (Edge Kitesport School: 01395 222551), surfing (Surfed Out: 01237 459445) and putting green
Parking	Pay parking (with disabled access) available
Information	Bideford Tourist Information Centre (01237 477676) or Torridge District Council (01237 428700)
Lifeguard Cover	May to September
Dogs	Restrictions from May to September
Useful Websites	www.devon-cornwall.co.uk www.visitdevon.co.uk

Saunton Sands

NEAREST TOWN BRAUNTON

Saunton Sands is an astonishing landscape, with a wide, 3 mile (5km) expanse of soft golden sands backed by Braunton Burrows, the UK's largest dune system, stretching inland as far as the eye can see. The beach's dramatic scale has long attracted film-makers – David Niven was washed up here in Powell and Pressburger's *A Matter of Life and Death* and Robbie Williams shot the Angels video here. The beach is packed in summer, its wide, west-facing, gently shelving shore making it an excellent surfing spot for novices.

At the north end the extensive white Saunton Sands Hotel overlooks the bay; at the southern end is Crow Point where the Taw and Torridge estuaries meet – this is a prime fishing site for bass, flounder, dabs and whiting, although it is dangerous for swimming.

You can sunbathe or find a quiet spot in the dunes of Braunton Burrows, an internationally important UNESCO biosphere reserve, with nearly 500 species of plants including orchids, water germander, sea stock and sand toadflax, as well as an abundance of unusual wildlife which includes more than 30 species of butterflies and the rare amber sandbowl snail. Saunton Sands is on the South West Coast Path – just around the next headland is Croyde Bay and beyond that rugged Baggy Point, a National Trust site, with views on a clear day to Pembrokeshire and the Gower Peninsular in Wales.

INFORMATION

Beach Type	Sand
Facilities	Toilets (with disabled facilities), shop and Sands Café Bar
Activities	Surf hire (Surfed Out: 01271 891286)
Parking	Pay parking available
Information	Braunton Tourist Information Centre (01271 816400)
Lifeguard Cover	None
Dogs	Restrictions apply between May and September
Useful Websites	www.devon-cornwall.co.uk
	www.visitdevon.co.uk
	www.brauntontic.co.uk

Beach Type	Sand
Facilities	Toilets (with disabled facilities and baby changing), cafés, shops, restaurants, pubs, hotels, B&Bs, beach huts and deck chair hire available
Activities	Surf hire and coaching (Hunter Surf School: 01271 871061 or Nick Thorn: 01271 871337), other outdoor activities available (H2Outdoor: 07789 807424)
Parking	Pay parking (with disabled access)
Information	Woolacombe Tourist Information Centre (01271 870553)
Lifeguard Cover	Easter to October
Dogs	Welcome on the middle and end section of the beach, some restrictions apply
Useful Websites	www.woolacombetourism.co.uk www.northdevon.com

Woolacombe Sands

NEAREST TOWN WOOLACOMBE

Woolacombe is an old-fashioned seaside town, with a beach that regularly makes it into the top ten British beach list. No wonder: 2½ miles (4km) of golden sand stretch between the headlands of Baggy Point and Morte Point, from where you get the best views of the lighthouse on Lundy Island 12 miles (19km) offshore. (You can take a day boat trip to Lundy from nearby Ilfracombe.)

The beach is backed by the sand dunes and heathland of Woolacombe Warren, and the downs where paragliders often take off. The west-facing beach gets a stiff breeze and is popular with surfers and windsurfers. It's one of Devon's best family destinations in summer, with wide sands for beach games, dunes for playing hide and seek, rock pools for marine life and a long row of quirkily painted beach huts.

Wander north along the shore and you come first to Barricane Beach, a sandy cove where pink and white cowrie shells are often washed up; then on to rocky Grunta Beach, so named because a shipload of pigs was once wrecked there. Just above this beach is the village of Mortehoe and the National Trust headland at Morte Point, where you can take guided tours by tractor and trailer.

Beach Type	Shingle and gravel
Facilities	Toilets (with disabled facilities) are available in the caravan park on the cliff-top, a shop and café are also available here. An ice cream van can be found on the access path to the beach during the summer months
Activities	None
Parking	Pay parking available at cliff top car park between March and October, a smaller winter car park is located at the entrance to the Holiday Park (01929 400200) and is free
Information	Wareham and Purbeck Tourist Information Centre (01929 552740)
Lifeguard Cover	None
Dogs	Welcome all year round
Useful Websites	www.visitswanageandpurbeck.com

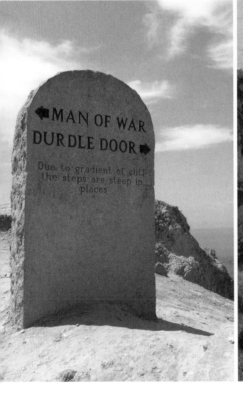 

Durdle Door
NEAREST TOWN WEST LULWORTH

Durdle Door is a place of wild, windswept grandeur where over centuries the seas have battered a massive arch through a hammerhead-shaped limestone headland. There's a steep path down from the South West Coast Path on the cliffs to the beach below, or at low tide you can walk along the beach from West Lulworth, a distance of a mile or so round St Oswald's Bay and Man O'War Head.

Durdle Door is part of the Jurassic Coast World Heritage site, and one of the many unusual geological formations in the area including Lulworth Cove, Chesil Beach and the Isle of Portland. The rocks here run vertically parallel with the coastline: originally a band of hard Portland limestone ran right along the shore, protecting the soft clay cliffs behind. But gradually, holes were punched in the limestone, and the sea quickly eroded the narrow band of clay – leaving Durdle Door standing in splendid isolation.

The beach is shingle, the sea glows aquamarine, and snorkellers and divers often explore the rocks, caves and arch. Swimming is possible although care is needed as the beach shelves sharply. Look out for fossils on the shoreline from the Jurassic and Cretaceous Periods up to 185 million years ago – ammonites, belemnites and dinosaur footprints are regularly found – but stay away from the cliff edges in case of rockfalls and landslides.

Swanage

NEAREST TOWN SWANAGE

The quaint, old-fashioned seaside resort of Swanage sits right at the eastern edge of the Isle of Purbeck. Originally a fishing village, it developed as a port in the 19th century when Purbeck limestone became a sought-after building material for newly developing industrial towns and cities. The ships went off laden with quarried stone, and returned with many curious stone and ironwork relics as ballast – including the town's Wellington Clock Tower.

Swanage also flourished as a Victorian seaside destination, with a glorious setting between chalk and limestone cliffs, a white sandy beach, pier and views past the sea stacks of Old Harry over to the Isle of Wight. Facing east, the bay is generally calm and sheltered, and good for swimming, sailing and scuba diving – this is a wreckers' coastline and there are many sunken ships to explore. Near the seafront there are deck chairs and pedal boats to hire, cafés, ice-cream kiosks, amusement arcades and a seasonal Punch and Judy show. You can take the restored steam railway to see the 1,000-year-old ruins of Corfe Castle, or walk along the South West Coast Path through Durlston Country Park to Durlston Head, with its 40-ton stone globe (erected in 1887). Continue past the former quarries of Tilly Whim caves (closed due to rockfalls) to Dancing Ledge, a rock shelf once used for loading Purbeck limestone, and now with a tidal swimming pool cut out of the rock in which you can take a lovely dip.

INFORMATION

Beach Type	Sand
Facilities	Toilets (with disabled facilities), several cafés and restaurants, first aid point and a lost child centre
Activities	A variety of watersports (Ocean Bay Watersports Centre: 01929 422224), fishing, crazy golf, boat charters (Swanage Boat Charters: 01929 427064) and diving (01929 423565)
Parking Information	Several car parks available in the area Swanage Tourist Information Centre (0870 4420680)
Lifeguard Cover	None, but there are beach wardens during the summer
Dogs	Welcome between October and April
Useful Websites	www.swanage.gov.uk

Studland

NEAREST TOWNS SWANAGE AND POOLE

Studland is one of the longest and most beautiful beaches in the country. East-facing and situated on the southern end of Poole Bay, its sheltered sands stretch 3 miles (5km) from the entrance to Poole Harbour down to Handfast Point, where the dramatic chalk sea stacks of Old Harry and his Wife can be seen offshore. There are spectacular views across to the Isle of Wight and the Needles; the white-gold sand is soft and the beach is an excellent spot for swimming, sandcastle building and sailing, with good cafés, watersports and other facilities. It's extremely busy in summer and becomes a bottleneck for traffic, so many visitors take the chain ferry from Poole, either on foot or by car.

The beach is divided into various areas: walk south from Shell Beach (where the ferry comes in; swimming is not recommended here due to estuarial tides) to Knoll Beach (which has a naturists' area and a NT tourist centre), then on to the sands of Middle Beach and the Redend Point Promontory. Below that is South Beach, which is cut off at high tides, where the sands narrow below the cliffs of Ballard Down.

Behind the beach is Studland Heath and a freshwater lake called Little Sea, both form part of a National Nature Reserve – a wild flower paradise and home to many unusual birds, lizards and even snakes.

INFORMATION	Beach Type	Sand
	Facilities	Toilets (including disabled facilities and baby changing), café, shops, boat park, Studland Study Centre (01929 450461) and a slipway to the beach. Beach huts are available for hire all year round (01929 450259)
	Activities	The National Trust provide activities on the beach, visit their website, details listed below
	Parking	There are four car parks available with various prices through the year. Disabled spaces are available at the Knoll car park
	Information	National Trust at Studland (01929 450259) or the Beach Ranger (07970 595963)
	Lifeguard Cover	None
	Dogs	Welcome from October to April, restrictions apply at other times
	Useful Websites	www.nationaltrust.org.uk

Beach Type	Sand
Facilities	Toilets (including disabled access and baby changing facilities), showers, first aid post, cafés and kiosk, beach wheelchairs/ beach huts/furniture also available for hire (Borough of Poole: 01202 708181)
Activities	Crazy golf, mini road train and watersports available (Poole Harbour Watersports: 01202 700503 and Jet Ski Safari: 07803 620650)
Parking	Pay parking available
Information	Poole Tourism (01202 253253)
Lifeguard Cover	May to September
Dogs	Restrictions on the main beach between May and September
Useful Websites	www.pooletourism.com

Sandbanks

NEAREST TOWN POOLE

Many people claim that Sandbanks is the best beach in Britain, its situation is certainly one of the most spectacular. The beach runs along the seaward side of a sand spit that stretches from the town of Poole across the mouth of Poole Harbour, just a stone's throw (and a short ferry ride) away from Shell Beach on the Isle of Purbeck. Poole Harbour is an Area of Outstanding Natural Beauty containing nature reserves and habitats that are home to many unusual species of birds and wildlife.

Sandbanks spit is low lying – much of it less than 10ft (3m) above sea level – with a narrow neck widening out to an area that totals less than 1sq mile (1sq km), and home to some of the country's most exclusive seaside houses and apartments. Sandbanks' south-east facing beach, a regular Blue Flag award-winner, is sheltered and extremely family-friendly, with golden sands gradually sloping into the water, which is safe for swimming. There are groynes to protect against sand drift and erosion, a promenade with cafés, shops, ice-cream kiosks, a crazy golf course, children's amusements and a mini road-train that gives rides along the seafront. The wide sands host volleyball and polo championships, and from the beach you can learn to windsurf and sail, or hire kayaks, jet-skis and inflatables. On the other side of the spit is Whitley Lake, a shallow part of the harbour recommended for board sailing, and the National Trust nature reserve at Brownsea Island, with its Sika deer, peacocks and red squirrels, just a short pedestrian ferry ride away.

Bournemouth Alum Chine

NEAREST TOWN BOURNEMOUTH

B ournemouth has 7 miles (11km) of golden sandy beaches fringed by wooded hills, but perhaps the prettiest and quietest is that of Alum Chine, well away from the crowds in the town centre. The beach is narrow, backed with a promenade and beach huts (which you can hire), and swimming on its gently shelving sands is extremely safe, with lifeguards throughout the summer season. It's a good family beach, with a paddling pool, pirate-themed children's playground (Robert Louis Stevenson, author of adventure and pirate stories, including *Treasure Island* and *Kidnapped*, lived in Bournemouth in the 1880s), shops and a café.

You can stroll through the gardens of the shady, wooded chine – the largest of Bournemouth's four chines where alum was once mined – and cross the three bridges across the valley for magnificent views of the coastline. It's a tranquil, historic spot: wander around the Tropical Gardens, laid out in the 1920s but replanted in the 1990s with a new viewing platform, to see the exotic banana trees, chusan palms, ginger lilies and agaves that thrive in the warm microclimate. There is also a terrace garden, tennis courts and a bowling green in the Argyll Gardens area of the chine.

INFORMATION

Beach Type	Sand
Facilities	Toilets (with disabled and baby changing facilities), first aid post, lost child centres, hotels, pubs, cafés/restaurants. Beach huts/ furniture available for hire (0845 0550968). Kid Zone safety scheme (children are issued with coloured wristbands)
Activities	There is a children's play area and a children's waterplay facility. The Land Train runs from Alum Chine to Bournemouth and from the Pier to Boscom Pier. Inflatable slides during the summer
Parking	Pay parking (with disabled access) available
Information	Bournemouth Tourist Information Centre (0845 0511700) or Seafront Office (01202 451781)
Lifeguard Cover	May to September
Dogs	Restrictions apply between May and September
Useful Websites	www.bournemouth.co.uk

Petit Bot Bay

NEAREST TOWN ST. PETER PORT

etit Bot Bay is situated on the dramatically rocky south coast of Guernsey, the second largest of the Channel Islands. It's a tiny bay cut into rough-hewn ochre cliffs that shelter it from strong winds. It's a glorious spot: two heavily wooded valleys, with a picturesque waterfall, run down to the beach. The road down cuts through a high wall on which a Martello defence tower stands, guarding the bay. There's also a coffee shop just at the entrance to the beach, converted from an old water mill with wheel.

At high tide the bay is indeed tiny but when the seas retreat a long expanse of fine, deep golden sand is revealed, with unusually shaped rock formations rising from the sands and waters beyond. You can see why Renoir liked it here – one of his most famous paintings was inspired by a nearby crop of rocks called the Pea Stacks (he also painted many scenes of nearby Moulin Huet Bay). The beach is very popular in summer as a sunbathing spot, and the craggy outcrops at either side are excellent for rock pool explorations. In the woods behind, you can walk for hours looking out for the many rare birds that summer here, including firecrests, great spotted woodpeckers, honey buzzards and golden orioles.

INFORMATION

Beach Type	Sand and rock
Facilities	Toilets (with disabled facilities), café, restaurant, slip way, first aid post and deck chair hire
Activities	No organised activities
Parking	Free parking available for 40 cars
Information	Visit Guernsey (01481 822994)
Lifeguard Cover	None
Dogs	Not permitted from May to September
Useful Websites	www.visitguernsey.com

TOP SPOTS FOR BIRDWATCHING

1 Bamburgh

2 West Wittering

3 Montrose

4 Marloes Sands

5 Petit Bot Bay

Miranda's favourites...

Beach Type	Sand
Facilities	Toilets, cafés and restaurants along the promenade
Activities	There are a large variety of watersports available, see Useful Websites for further listings
Parking	Free parking available
Information	Jersey Tourist Information Centre (01534 448800)
Lifeguard Cover	May to September
Dogs	Must be kept on a lead between 10am and 6pm from May to September
Useful Websites	www.jersey.com

St. Brelade's Bay

NEAREST TOWN ST. BRELADE

St. Brelade's is Jersey's busiest beach but it's also one of the most beautiful. It sits on the island's south coast, a huge, horseshoe-shaped bay protected from the elements by a large headland. The sands are soft and golden, and the tides race out for miles leaving a huge expanse of beach – head east and walk right the way round to neighbouring Ouaisne Bay at low tide. St. Brelade's calm, clear waters make it a haven for safe swimming and water sports. You can hire pedalos and kayaks, take a trip around the bay in a speedboat or by hanging on to a banana boat, play volleyball or trampoline on the foreshore, or relax in one of the many cafés around the bay.

It's the perfect place for a family beach day out, with exciting wildlife walks around the coastal cliffs in either direction – you might see red squirrels, blue-winged grasshoppers, stonechats, linnets, Dartford warblers and a wide range of wild plants, such as sand crocus, bird's foot trefoil and golden rod. St. Brelade's even has some history: tucked into the most westerly corner are the 12th-century parish church of St. Brelade and next door Fishermen's Chapel, with its exquisite 14th-century wall paintings of biblical scenes.

Corblets

NEAREST TOWN ST. ANNE

Tiny Alderney, just 3½ miles (5.5km) long by a mile or so wide, and the third largest of the Channel Islands, is very close to the French coast and has been of great strategic and military importance over the ages. As a result, almost every beach on the island has either a Victorian or German fortification. Corblets is no exception: the imposing ramparts of 19th-century Fort Corblets overlook the eastern end of the sheltered, sandy bay. From the fort there are steep steps down to the beach, which has clear blue seas and golden sand, with rocky outcrops and a rich variety of marine life, making it an excellent spot for scouring rock pools. The beach faces the English Channel but is protected from easterly winds, and is the best surfing, windsurfing and body-boarding spot on the island – even better, it's often blissfully quiet and uncrowded. Swimming is safe, and at high tide you can dive into the sea from the rocks below the fort, a rare treat.

Corblets is a wonderful beach for families but take your binoculars too – it's a haven for wildlife enthusiasts, with an unusually wide variety of flora and fauna. On the craggy coastal footpaths, look out for some of the 270 bird species found on Alderney, plus unusual animals and invertebrates such as rare blonde hedgehogs, greater white tooth shrews, soprano and Nathusius' pipistrelle bats, gatekeeper butterflies and tiny, yellow-tummied Alderney bees.

Beach Type	Sand
Facilities	None on the beach, there is the Saye camp site (01481 822556) nearby which has a small shop and tearoom
Activities	No organised activities, although it is a very popular surf spot
Parking	Free parking available
Information	Alderney Tourist Information Centre (01481 822994)
Lifeguard Cover	None
Dogs	Not welcome between 1st May and 30th September
Useful Websites	www.visitalderney.com www.alderneywildlife.org

INFORMATION

Beach Type	Sand
Facilities	None
Activities	No organised activities
Parking	None
Information	St. Mary's Tourist Information Centre (01720 422536)
Lifeguard Cover	None
Dogs	Welcome all year
Useful Websites	www.simplyscilly.co.uk

The Bar and Cove Vean

NEAREST TOWN ST. AGNES

Once you've reached the main island of St. Mary's, it's a short boat trip to St. Agnes, the wildest and least changed of the five inhabited Isles of Scilly. This is a quiet, peaceful place, even in the height of summer. Disembarking at the quay at Porth Conger, follow the track uphill past the island's only and excellent pub, The Turk's Head – try the delicious Cornish pasties while you're there. Take the small track down to the narrow sandbank called The Bar: at low tide you can walk across to the tiny isle of Gugh (pronounced 'Hugh'). Here you'll find remarkable Bronze Age remains including a 10ft (3m) standing stone called the Old Man of Gugh, overlooking St. Mary's, and Obadiah's Barrow, a prehistoric burial chamber.

Back over The Bar, head a little south and down a leafy path you'll find Cove Vean, a wonderful sandy beach and deep-water cove, framed by rocky outcrops. You can swim in the clear, aquamarine sea and snorkel among the rocks that bustle with marine life. If you're lucky you'll see bass and, on land, the Scilly shrew (right), a rare, long-nosed shrew that forages in hedgerows and beaches on the island.

Pentle Bay

NEAREST TOWN TRESCO

Pentle Bay is the longest and widest beach on the isle of Tresco, stretching from Tobaccoman's Point ¾ mile (1.2km) north to Lizard Point, with views of the remote eastern isles and St. Martin's to the north-east. In the dunes leading down to the beach, purply blue agapanthus – a South African native plant – grow wild among the marram grass, and speckled wood and clouded yellow butterflies flutter around. The beach is one of Britain's best for families, its clear sapphire waters safe for swimming and snorkelling, and its powdery white sands full of beautiful and unusual shells for beachcombers. Boats bob along the coastline, some casting anchor on the sparkling shores of the bay – it's paradise on earth.

A little way inland you will reach Great Pool, a huge freshwater pond that slashes across almost the width of the island. In autumn it's a utopia for bird-watchers, attracting plovers, pipits and wagtails as well as rare species such as great northern divers, pectoral sandpipers, red-backed shrikes and firecrests. Follow the track (Tresco is almost car-free – feet, bikes and golf buggies are mostly used to get around) between Great Pool and Abbey Pool and you come to Tresco Abbey, a house built above the site of the ruined St. Nicholas Priory by the Isles of Scilly's Lord Proprietor Augustus Smith in the 19th century. You can get to Tresco by helicopter from Penzance, or by boat from the main island of St. Mary's.

Beach Type	Sand
Facilities	None
Activities	None
Parking	None
Information	Isles of Scilly Tourist Information Centre (01720 422536) or Tresco Estate (01720 422849)
Lifeguard Cover	None
Dogs	Welcome all year, but must be kept on a lead
Useful Websites	www.tresco.co.uk

Bryher
NEAREST TOWN BRYHER

The tiny island of Bryher, the smallest of the five Isles of Scilly, is a mile long and just half a mile wide, and a natural wilderness of incredible scenic contrasts. In the northwest, the Atlantic rollers roar and gurgle over the rocks at the aptly named Hell Bay, with spray leaping 40ft (12m) high over the headland in stormy weather. Yet walk a few hundred yards along the sandy lanes to the eastern seaboard and you come to two tranquil beaches, where turquoise waters lap on to blazingly white sands and exotic plants abound – you could almost be in the tropics. Green Bay has views over to the palm trees of Tresco's Abbey Gardens – indeed you can wade the channel between the islands at very low tides. A little further south is Rushy Bay, a beautiful beach facing the narrow strip of sea to the deserted island of Samson, and the place where boats have to come in at low tide.

Fewer than 100 people live on Bryher; there are few roads and fewer vehicles and only the distant echo of a tractor or boat will break the tranquillity. Near Hell Bay, one of England's most westerly points, you get glorious sunsets across the open seas to America, and might even catch the elusive 'green flash' as the sun finally goes down. There's a luxury hotel in a converted cowshed (Hell Bay Hotel), a gallery, cafés, and food and farm shops selling locally grown produce, where they trust you to leave the money in the pot. It's that kind of place.

INFORMATION

Beach Type	Sand
Facilities	None
Activities	None
Parking	None
Information	Isles of Scilly Tourist Information Centre (01720 422536)
Lifeguard Cover	None
Dogs	Welcome all year
Useful Websites	www.bryher-ios.co.uk
	www.simplyscilly.co.uk

south east

The English Channel and Straits of Dover, stretching along the coastlines of Hampshire, Sussex and Kent, form one of the world's busiest commercial shipping areas. There are huge natural harbours and ports at Southampton, Portsmouth and Chichester, and it's fascinating to watch the sailing boats go by in the busy Solent (good views from Seagrove Bay) or around East Head into Chichester Harbour (from West Wittering). The coast of Hampshire is relatively short – 34 miles (54km) as the crow flies – but the resort and sailing destinations of the Isle of Wight and Hayling Island give it an irresistible holiday atmosphere.

The Sussex coast is mostly built up from Bognor Regis to Brighton and Newhaven, but there's a wonderful stretch past Seaford where the white chalk South Downs meet the sea. This is the Seven Sisters – a series of spectacular white cliff peaks – and Beachy Head, the highest chalk cliff in England at 534ft (162m). You can see the lonely lighthouse below, dwarfed by the cliffs, and there are views west to the Isle of Wight and east as far as the flat and beautiful shingle headland of Dungeness.

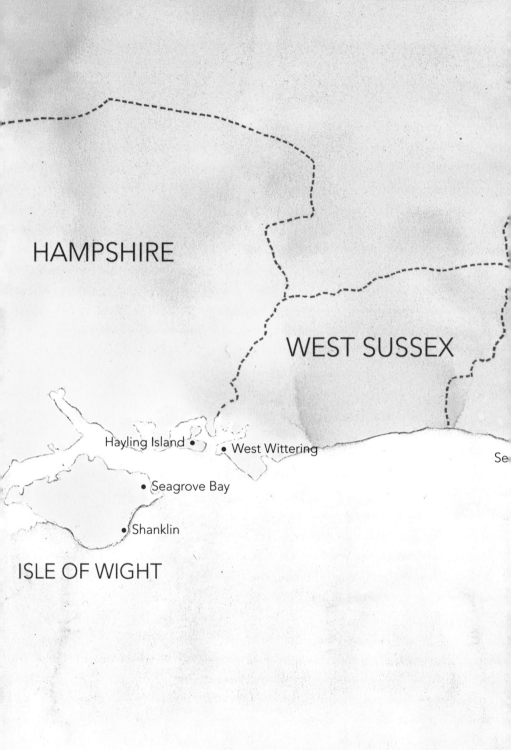

HAMPSHIRE

WEST SUSSEX

Hayling Island •

• West Wittering

Se

• Seagrove Bay

• Shanklin

ISLE OF WIGHT

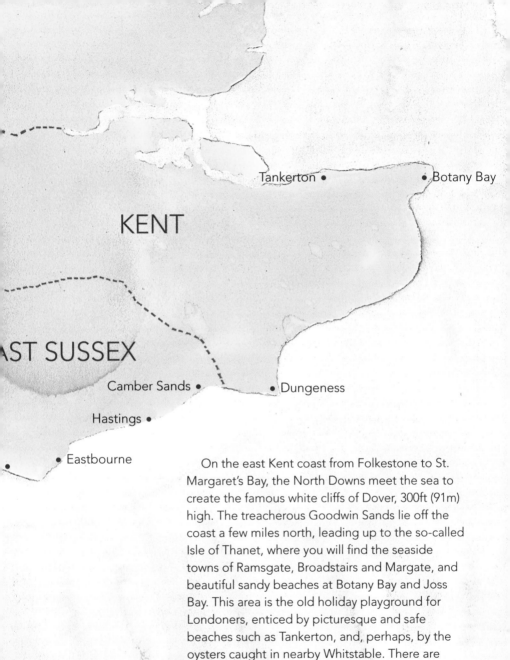

Tankerton •   • Botany Bay

KENT

\ST SUSSEX

Camber Sands •   • Dungeness

Hastings •

• Eastbourne

On the east Kent coast from Folkestone to St. Margaret's Bay, the North Downs meet the sea to create the famous white cliffs of Dover, 300ft (91m) high. The treacherous Goodwin Sands lie off the coast a few miles north, leading up to the so-called Isle of Thanet, where you will find the seaside towns of Ramsgate, Broadstairs and Margate, and beautiful sandy beaches at Botany Bay and Joss Bay. This area is the old holiday playground for Londoners, enticed by picturesque and safe beaches such as Tankerton, and, perhaps, by the oysters caught in nearby Whitstable. There are interesting coast paths around the whole region, especially the Saxon Shore Way that takes you 160 miles (257km) along the old Roman coastline (some of it now inland) from Hastings to Gravesend.

Beach Type	Sand
Facilities	Toilets (with disabled facilities), shops, cafés and a promenade
Activities	Windsurfing, surfing, kayaking and sailing
Parking	Limited parking available, further parking at Seaview Village which is a short walk away
Information	Newport Tourist Information Centre (01983 813818)
Lifeguard Cover	None
Dogs	Restrictions between May and September
Useful Websites	www.isleofwight.com

Seagrove Bay
NEAREST TOWN RYDE

Situated on the north-eastern tip of the Isle of Wight between Ryde and St. Helens, Seagrove Bay is something of a hidden gem. The bay is tucked away and is only accessible by foot through the pretty fishing village of Seaview. Its secluded situation, and the nearby Edwardian villas inland make it reminiscent of an England long gone by – even the local tourist authority calls it old-fashioned. The beach is shingle from the sea wall to the high-tide line, with rocks and golden sands below when the tide goes out. It's a place to enjoy the sun, sand, sea (it's safe for swimming) and, with nets and buckets, the rocks that children love to climb on. The views from Seagrove are spectacular, not only of the bright blue water of the Solent but also of the 19th-century St. Helen's Fort sitting just offshore. The coast around Seaview is protected under the European Birds Directive and in nearby Hersey Nature Reserve there's a hide where you can see egrets, greenshanks, shelducks, water rails, herons. If it's peace and tranquillity you're after, this is the place to find it.

✓ good

Shanklin ✓

NEAREST TOWN SHANKLIN

Where Seagrove is quiet, Shanklin, on the east coast of the Isle of Wight, is positively throbbing with life. The bay lies beneath 150ft (45.5m) cliffs with the picturesque Shanklin Chine, a wooded coastal ravine with gardens, streams and waterfalls, which are spectacularly lit up at night, running through. But it's the beach below that really attracts visitors. It's sheltered from prevailing winds by the cliffs at Luccombe and Dunnose Point to the south, with views around to Bembridge and the chalk cliffs at Culver. The golden sands are lapped by bright blue waters and somehow, in this southerly part of the country, the weather always seems to be on your side. The beach is regularly cleaned during the summer, even the seaweed is removed (to be used as compost by local farmers), and it has Blue Flag-winning waters and lifeguards patrolling. It's quietest at the southern end where you will find the Fisherman's Cottage pub which is well worth a visit for the food and the ambience. Head north towards Sandown for bustling shops, cafés and amusements. An esplanade with pitch and putt, children's amusements and a small road train links the two areas, and there is a lift to the top of the cliffs, if you don't want to use the steps. There's also Shanklin's fascinating 'old village' to the south, with higgledy-piggledy thatched houses with pretty cottage gardens, gift shops, pubs such as the renowned Crab Inn, and tearooms where you can get real cream teas and try out the local sea catches.

MARVELLOUS
IM

PLENTY

INFORMATION

Beach Type	Sand
Facilities	Toilets (with disabled facilities), café, restaurants, lost child centre, a variety of shops, first aid post, hotels along the front, lift up and down the cliff face, several slipways and beach huts available for hire (01983 813813)
Activities	Sailing (Shanklin Sailing Club: 01983 528478), pitch and putt, children's amusements and Vectis Road Train during the summer months
Parking	Pay parking (with disabled access)
Information	Countryside Parks and Beaches Department (01983 823893)
Lifeguard Cover	May to October
Dogs	Not permitted between May and September
Useful websites	www.isleofwight.com

Hayling Island

NEAREST TOWN PORTSMOUTH

Despite sitting very close to the east coast of Portsmouth, Hayling Island is mostly a serene place. There's one road on and off the island, from Havant, which runs from North Hayling to the shingle and sand beaches of South Hayling, through a lovely conservation area full of rare flowers and plants. You can walk all the way along the sands facing south to the Solent from West Beach to Sandy Point in the east. Along the way, there are beach huts at Bound Lane which, the local council claims, is the birthplace of windsurfing. (In fact, there's a permanent surf camera on the island, which is accessible online so that you can check when the big waves are coming.) Head to West Beach for the best swimming in the 'lagoon' that forms naturally because the beach is sheltered by a sandbar (it is of Blue Flag standard). Disturbing the peace a little is Funland at Beachlands (just east of the West Beach), an old-fashioned seaside amusement park complete with roller-coaster and log ride, and you can find holiday camps and good fish and chips at Eastoke Beach. From the island's most easterly spot at Sandy Point you can watch the sailboats in Chichester harbour and the Witterings. But don't bathe here, the tides can be treacherous.

Beach Type	Shingle
Facilities	Toilets (with disabled facilities), kiosks, cafés, a first aid post and beach patrol
Activities	There are three golf courses nearby, donkeys are available on the beach during the summer and a variety of watersports are available (02392 422570)
Parking	Free parking (with disabled access) available from November to March, pay parking for the rest of the year
Information	Hayling Island Tourist Information Centre (02392 467111)
Lifeguard Cover	Coast guard all year round
Dogs	Not permitted on West Beach from Good Friday to October
Useful Websites	www.havant.gov.uk

Beach Type	Sand
Facilities	Toilets (with disabled facilities and baby changing), showers, first aid post, lost child centre, kiosks and a café, beach furniture is available for hire (01243 514143)
Activities	A variety of watersport activities available (West Wittering Windsurfing Club: 01243 513077)
Parking	Pay parking (with disabled access) available
Information	Chichester Tourist Information Centre (01243 775888)
Lifeguard Cover	May to September
Dogs	From May to September, dogs are excluded from the main swimming beach between groynes 14a to 18. They are welcome during the remainder of the year.
Useful Websites	www.westwitteringbeach.co.uk www.chichesterweb.co.uk

West Wittering
NEAREST TOWN CHICHESTER

In an area noted for its sailing, West Wittering offers a quiet place from which to watch the yachts go by. It's part of a privately owned estate, accessible only via a toll road, but there is extensive parking close to the sands. The beach itself is beautiful: the golden sand is intercut with numbered groynes and, although it's popular with local windsurfers and kitesurfers, there's plenty of room to swim without bumping into boats or boards. The 156 beach huts that line the shore are privately owned, so go prepared to change under a towel.

At the western end of the beach lies East Head, a 24 acre (10 hectare) sand dune spit that curves into Chichester Harbour, which is accessible only by a very narrow strip of sand known as 'the hinge'. This fragile eco-system (managed by the National Trust) is a Site of Special Scientific Interest and a bird-watchers' paradise, enclosing wetlands and reedbeds where you can see a range of waterbirds including plovers, redshanks, egrets, herons, sanderlings, curlews and oystercatchers. West Wittering beach is clean and tidy and the quality of the water is of a high standard. You feel very close to nature here.

INFORMATION

Beach Type	Shingle
Facilities	Toilets (including disabled facilities), café, first aid post, camp site and caravan park (01323 897801), kiosks, beach huts available to rent (01323 894870)
Activities	Sailing (Newhaven and Seaford Sailing Club: 01323 890077), Donkey Derby in August
Parking	Free parking available next to the beach
Information	Seaford Tourist Information Centre (01323 897426)
Lifeguard Cover	Weekends between April and September
Dogs	Restricted access between April and September
Useful Websites	www.enjoysussex.info

Seaford Bay

NEAREST TOWN SEAFORD

S ituated about 10 miles (16km) east of Brighton, near the mouth of the River Ouse and facing south-west, Seaford's beach can be spectacularly wild when the weather is bad. It was devastated by the great storm of 1987 and has since been completely rebuilt, with an esplanade and sea wall to protect the town from flooding. The shingle beach stretches over 2 miles (3km) from Tide Mills – a ruined 18th-century mill village – via the Buckle, the site of a bloody battle with the French in 1545, to Splash Point and the chalk cliffs at Seaford Head above.

Seaford Head is a nature reserve, with a breeding colony of kittiwakes and spectacular views – you can also visit the remains of an Iron Age fort and watch hang gliders taking off from the 300ft (91m) high cliffs. The town has a vibrant history: in medieval times it was a thriving port, a 'limb' of the Cinque Port of Hastings, but shingle drift blocked the river mouth and trading moved to Newhaven. When the railways arrived in the 19th century, Seaford became a popular seaside resort instead. Today, it's a quiet, family destination, with good walks in the nearby Seven Sisters Country Park and bird-watching in the Ouse Estuary Nature Reserve. There's also the Martello Tower no. 74, the last in a chain built to protect the south coast from Napoleonic attack, which now houses Seaford museum. While the swimming is good here, note that there's a steep drop not far out of the bay, so care is needed.

Eastbourne

NEAREST TOWN EASTBOURNE

Ever since 1780, when King George III's children began to take their summer holidays in the town, Eastbourne has held the reputation of being the English resort for the discerning visitor. Approached by sea in early evening, the elegant, white-stuccoed Georgian and early Victorian houses along the seafront could be mistaken for a continuation of nearby Beachy Head's chalk cliffs, hung with pretty, twinkling lights. The shingle and sand (at low tide) beach at Eastbourne is clean, evenly cut by groynes and bordered by a promenade with well-stocked flowerbeds – put your sunglasses on to view them – and lush grassy areas. The stretch of beach from the Victorian pier (which contains a camera obscura) to Wish Tower is of a Blue Flag standard. To the east of the pier you can walk towards Langney Point a couple of miles away. Along the Royal Parade stands the Redoubt Fortress & Military Museum, an impressive circular fortress built to defend the south coast against Napoleonic attack, now housing military collections and exhibitions. North-east of the pier there's Princes Park, with putting and bowling greens, playgrounds, a model boating lake and flower gardens, all confirming Eastbourne as one of the most genteel seaside resorts in the country.

INFORMATION

Beach Type	Sand, shingle and pebbles
Facilities	Cafés, restaurants, shops, lost child centre, first aid post, slipway, showers, toilets (with disabled facilities), pier, bandstand, beach huts and furniture for hire (Seafront Office: 01323 410611)
Activities	A variety of watersports available (Spray Watersports: 01323 417023 or the Sailing and Windsurfing Club: 01323 720715)
Parking	Pay and free parking available along the seafront (with disabled access)
Information	Eastbourne Tourist Information Centre (0871 6630031) or Seafront Office (01323 410611)
Lifeguard Cover	June to September
Dogs	From May to September dogs must be kept on leads and are banned from the main resort beach
Useful Websites	www.visiteastbourne.com

TOP SPOTS FOR FOSSILS

1 Hastings
2 Frinton-on-Sea
3 Robin Hood's Bay
4 Brora
5 Durdle Door

Miranda's
favourites...

Hastings

NEAREST TOWN HASTINGS

Hastings is an ancient town, one of the original, medieval Cinque Ports, and the site of a castle built by William the Conqueror after the invasion of 1066 (the Battle of Hastings itself was fought 8 miles (13km) away at Senlac Hill). The shoreline is shingle at high tide, but large expanses of golden sand are revealed when the tide goes out, and the town is fringed by dramatic steep cliffs behind.

The beach has something for everyone. At the Pelham end, bordering the neighbouring town of St. Leonard's, there is a Victorian pier and all the traditional attractions of a family seaside resort – a promenade, boating lake, amusements, cafés and miniature railway.

Further east, in front of Hastings old town – where many half-timbered buildings such as Ye Olde Pumpe House in George Street date from the 15th century – there's Stade beach, with its harbour arm to give protection to fishing boats. Hastings has the largest beach-based fishing fleet in England, and the picturesque clinkerbuilt boats, made with overlapping wooden planks, berth on the sands at low tide. Hastings modest fleet of 27 boats is one of just six UK fisheries to gain Marine Conservation Society accreditation, and it is the only fishery in the world so far to gain the MSC's internationally recognised eco-label, for its sole, as well as fishing sustainable mackerel and herring.

Beach Type	Sand and shingle	
Facilities	Toilets, shops, cafés, restaurants, first aid, lost child centre, promenade and pier. Deck chair hire is available	
Activities	The pier provides a selection of entertainment. Trampolines during the summer and Cliff Railways (01424 781030) is worth a visit	
Parking	A variety of car parks are available	
Information	Hastings Tourist Information Centre (0845 2741001)	
Lifeguard Cover	May to September	
Dogs	Restrictions between May and September	
Useful Websites	www.hastings.gov.uk/beaches www.1066country.com	

Camber Sands

NEAREST TOWN RYE

No wonder Camber Sands is often used as a location for films and fashion shoots – its towering sand dunes and 2 mile (3km) long golden beach make a fantastic backdrop. Children love rolling and jumping in the high dunes, and when the tide goes out for up to half a mile, it leaves a broad, open expanse of sand that you can play the wildest beach games on. Even at the height of the summer season, when visitors flood in from the town's many holiday parks, you can still find a quiet spot to put down your towel. Although, beware of the fast-returning tide – you can get stranded if you're not careful. Kite-boarding and kite-buggying are both popular at the eastern end of the beach. The dunes are a designated area of scientific interest, there are lots of dog-free areas and, as long as the sea is calm, swimming is good. It's about two hours from London and a good walk or brief drive from Rye Harbour, with lovely views across the Romney Marshes.

INFORMATION

Beach Type	Sand
Facilities	Toilets (including disabled facilities), café, restaurants, shops, first aid post, lost child centre, slip way, camp site and caravan park (01797 225756), windbreaks for hire
Activities	A variety of watersports available (Lydd Watersports: 01797 320179)
Parking	Several car parks available, all pay and display
Information	Rye Tourist Information Centre (01797 226696)
Lifeguard Cover	None
Dogs	Restricted access, but clearly signposted at the beach
Useful Websites	www.visitrye.co.uk

INFORMATION

Beach Type	Shingle
Facilities	The railway station at Dungeness has a café and toilets
Activities	The Old Lighthouse is open for visitors (01797 321300)
Parking	Free parking
Information	Romney, Hythe and Dymchurch Railway (01797 362353)
Lifeguard Cover	There is a lifeboat station
Dogs	Welcome, but restrictions apply
Useful Websites	www.heartofkent.org.uk

Dungeness
NEAREST TOWN LYDD

Not everyone understands the allure of Dungeness. This is a strange and weirdly beautiful place, and the largest shingle formation in the world, except for Cape Canaveral in Florida, set on a windswept promontory that juts into the English Channel. Filmmaker Derek Jarman made something of a tourist attraction of the area, creating an unusual garden at Prospect Cottage, an old fisherman's cottage that he made his home. Across the expanse of shingle there are unobstructed views of two architecturally dramatic nuclear power stations (one decommissioned), two lighthouses and the flats of Romney Marshes inland. There's a rich range of unusual vegetation and wildlife – including stoats, marsh frogs, weasels and bats – and the bird-watching is excellent. Near the RSPB visitor centre there are six hides, and you're likely to see kingfishers, warblers, bitterns, smew, grebes and wheatears, depending on the season.

There are a couple of pubs and a café at the station for the steam railway, which runs from Hythe to Dungeness, in case hunger strikes. Walking on the heavy shingle is tough on the legs, and swimming is inadvisable off this coast. Instead, enjoy the wildlife and be awestruck by this beautiful, otherworldly terrain.

Botany Bay
NEAREST TOWN BROADSTAIRS

Seated at the foot of chalk cliffs, halfway around the Isle of Thanet headland between Victorian Broadstairs (one of Charles Dickens' favoured holiday spots) and Margate, sits a sandy beach dotted with rocks at low tide. It's named Botany Bay – and it's not the only one, even in England. (There are others in Chorley, Monmouthshire, Enfield and Bristol, as well as the infamous BB in the antipodes.) Botany Bay is the most northerly of seven bays around Broadstairs, each with their own particular character. It's a beautiful setting, with milky blue sea, golden sands, chalk-white cliffs and astonishing rock formations, giving an almost tropical ambience to the beach. Access is on foot by steps or ramp, and there's a little kiosk at the bottom where you can buy tea, coffee, ice-cream and snacks, as well as hire windbreaks. But despite this social hub, the beach is generally quiet and swimming is safe, with lifeguards from mid-June to September. There's a wealth of seashells and marine life to be found in the chalky rockpools, including crabs, piddocks, cuttlefish and starfish. Make sure you take a net, bucket and spade – this is a smashing beach for a family day out.

INFORMATION

Beach Type	Sand
Facilities	Toilets (with disabled facilities), first aid, lost child centre and a café/restaurant, windbreaks for hire
Activities	Surfing and canoeing are popular here
Parking	Available on the roadside at the top of the cliffs. Disabled spaces available.
Information	Broadstairs Tourist Information Centre (0870 2646111) or Foreshore Department (01843 577274)
Lifeguard Cover	May to September
Dogs	Not permitted from May to September between 10am and 6pm, but welcome during the winter months
Useful Websites	www.visitthanet.co.uk

Tankerton

NEAREST TOWN WHITSTABLE

Tankerton beach is situated to the east of Whitstable old town, with its weatherboarded buildings, sail lofts, boathouses and, most famously, oysters. At Tankerton, gentle grassy slopes – perfect for summer picnics – roll down from the houses and hotels on Marine Parade to meet rows of colourful beach huts along the seafront. The beach is shingle, often built up between the groynes due to wind and high waves. At low tide, you can walk on a natural causeway called 'The Street' – a long shingle spit leading out to sea (though be careful to beat the tide when it's coming back in).

The bay faces slightly west, so the sunsets are sensational, with views over the Thames estuary to Southend and the Isle of Sheppey. Perhaps because of the rolling grassy slopes, the beach has a gentle, rural feel. It's well known for sailing and the swimming is good. For the past 200 years, there's been a summer regatta on Tankerton slopes to celebrate the fishing and oystercatching tradition of the area – everyone gets together for a funfair, stalls and fireworks. The path along the beach forms part of the Saxon Shore Way, a walking route that traces the eastern coastline as it was in Roman days (Romans famously liked the oysters too).

Beach Type	Pebbles
Facilities	Toilets (with disabled facilities) and a café
Activities	No organised activities
Parking	Free on-street parking available
Information	Foreshore Office (01227 266719)
Lifeguard Cover	May to September
Dogs	Not permitted between May and September
Useful Websites	www.visitcanterbury.co.uk

east

The 250 mile (402km) coastline from the Thames
estuary to the Wash is dotted with river inlets
and channels, secluded creeks, unspoilt sand
and shingle beaches, mud flats, salt marshes,
shingle spits and low, crumbling cliffs. The Essex
beaches of Southend, Leigh-on-Sea and Frinton-
on-Sea are fine and sandy, but between them the
low-lying coast is deeply indented by a series of
large, twisting rivers and estuaries that make this
area one of Britain's finest for sailing – the annual
Burnham-on-Crouch regatta is known as the
'Cowes of the east'.

North past Harwich, the beaches have coarse,
reddish sand and boast a treasure trove of unusual
stones such as jet, carnelian, jasper and agate –
you might even find small pieces of amber.
The long, shingle, vegetated spit at Orford Ness
is the largest in Europe, but like most of this
coastline is under threat of erosion by rising sea
levels and longshore drift – indeed the nearby
village of Dunwich has almost completely
disappeared. Much of the Suffolk coastline is quiet
and relatively undeveloped, although the busy,
old-fashioned seaside towns of Aldeburgh,

Thorpeness, Walberswick and Southwold, all with their own beaches (some shingle, some sandy), have traditional resort attractions.

From Great Yarmouth around north-east Norfolk's huge coastline curve is a magnificent stretch of golden sand, in many places backed by low, crumbling cliffs, where sand martins nest. Inland are the protected wetlands, marshes and inland waterways of the Norfolk and Suffolk Broads, a holiday destination and a sanctuary for rare plants and wildlife. Past the sand and shingle beach of Sheringham, and stretching almost to Hunstanton, is a shifting, marshland coastline of mud flats, reed beds and salt marshes, with huge and beautiful sandy beaches at Holkham and Wells-next-the-Sea. The many nature reserves here provide a wilderness haven for birds such as avocets, oystercatchers, bitterns and terns, while off the 3 mile (5km) sand and shingle spit of Blakeney Point you can see large colonies of grey and common seals.

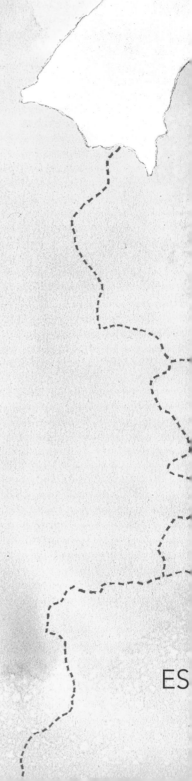

ES

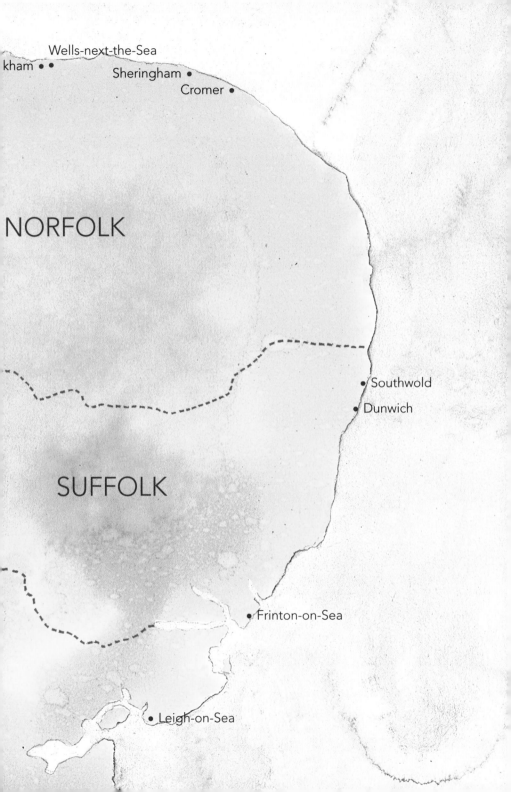

Leigh-on-Sea

NEAREST TOWN SOUTHEND-ON-SEA

Next to the amusements, lights and gaudy attractions of Southend, the small cobbled streets of Leigh-on-Sea, at the eastern end of Southend's built-up seafront, retain an old-world charm. The beach is sandy, bordered by a railway line and a pathway, and it's possible to walk along the 7 mile (11km) stretch of beach from Leigh via Southend to Shoeburyness, just around the headland. When the tide recedes, huge expanses of mudflats stretch out into the Thames estuary, with sailing boats left high and dry. But when the tide comes in, the beach is excellent for swimming, windsurfing and sailing, and just mucking around on the sand.

Leigh is famous for its cockles, oysters and jellied eels. Visit Cockle Row between the old town and the station, where there are many traditional weatherboarded seafood sheds selling locally caught seafood – delicious and cheap. The town is set on a hill, which you can climb for great views of the sea, Canvey Island and Kent to the south. Leigh-on-Sea is a peaceful, charming resort and a refuge, if you need one, from the roar of the one-armed bandits just down the road.

INFORMATION	Beach Type	Sand
	Facilities	The beach is in a town so has use of the varied facilities like toilets, shops, cafés and restaurants
	Activities	Heritage museum (01702 470834), Lynn Tate Gallery (01702 471737) and the Sailing Club (01702 476788). This is a popular beach for watersports
	Parking	Limited parking on the beach, however, further parking in the town is available
	Information	Southend Tourist Information Centre (01702 215620)
	Lifeguard Cover	None
	Dogs	Banned from 1st May to 30th September
	Useful Websites	www.leigh-on-sea.com

INFORMATION

Beach Type	Sand
Facilities	Slip-way and toilets (including disabled facilities)
Activities	Visit www.essex-sunshine-coast.org.uk for full activity and event listings
Parking	Free parking available on the promenade (with disabled access)
Information	Walton Tourist Information Centre (01255 675542)
Lifeguard Cover	Summer patrols from July to September
Dogs	Restrictions from May to September on certain stretches of the beach, these will be clearly marked
Useful Websites	www.essex-sunshine-coast.org.uk

Frinton-on-Sea

NEAREST TOWN FRINTON-ON-SEA

Situated on the north-east Essex coast, between the working port of Harwich and the brash seaside entertainments of Clacton, Frinton is charmingly caught in time somewhere in the mid-1950s. The town was laid out in the early 20th century, with broad, tree-lined avenues stretching towards the beach, and you can find some of the country's finest examples of 1930s modernist houses here, with their flat roofs and streamlined, ocean-liner-like facades. The main route into town leads visitors over a manually operated railway crossing, which only confirms the feeling that this is a place of timelessness, secluded from the modern world.

The beach, which is sandy and golden when the tide is out, is approached across a wide greensward. On a sea wall above runs a mile-long promenade, peppered with rows of Victorian-type beach huts. Until very recently, there were no pubs at all and, since the local council refuses to give licences to street traders near the beach, there is no litter – and no ice cream to be had unless you head back over the greensward. Forget modern amusements – this is a wonderful place to enjoy traditional fun and games on the beach, armed with just a bucket and spade and a picnic. Just a short walk east to the neighbouring beach of Walton-on-the-Naze you'll find the best fossils in Essex, the crumbling cliffs revealing sharks' teeth, gastropods and bivalves up to 50 million years old.

Dunwich

NEAREST TOWN SOUTHWOLD

The town of Dunwich has been a victim of rising tides for centuries. Seven hundred years ago a tidal wave ruined the harbour of what was then one of England's most important ports. In the centuries since, the erosion of the coast has removed almost all traces of the once-thriving town's many churches, chapels, houses and hospitals, leaving just one inn, one church, the Dunwich Museum and a few scattered houses – remarkably these would have stood more than a mile inland in medieval times.

Dunwich is still a curiosity well worth visiting. The shingled beach leads visitors along a changing cliff face, worn away daily by the elements. On occasion, you can even see skeletons exposed in the cliffs from ancient graveyards and, if you search carefully, you can find eroded remains of long-lost buildings on the beach. You can see the nuclear power station at Sizewell in the southern distance; there's some some fantastic bird-watching to be done on Dunwich Heath, where the salt water is flooding into the inland marshes; and fresh doughnuts to be eaten at the black weatherboarded Flora Tea Rooms in the beach car park. The National Trust runs the Dunwich Heath Beach and Coastal Area, and organises many excellent child-centred activities in the summer.

INFORMATION	**Beach Type**	Shingle
	Facilities	Toilets (with disabled facilities) and a café
	Activities	The National Trust runs activities during the summer season
	Parking	Pay parking available
	Information	Aldeburgh Tourist Information Centre (01728 453637)
	Lifeguard Cover	None
	Dogs	Occasional restrictions during the nesting season, contact the RSPB for further details (01728 648281)
	Useful Websites	www.dunwich.ukfossils.co.uk www.nationaltrust.org.uk

INFORMATION

Beach Type	Sand and shingle
Facilities	Toilets (with disabled access), shops, cafés, a pier, putting green and a lost child centre
Activities	Sailing club (01502 725201), Coastal Voyager excursion (07887 525082) all year round and a yearly sandcastle competition, judged by the mayor.
Parking	Pay parking during summer (free during winter)
Information	Southwold Tourist Information Centre (01502 724729)
Lifeguard Cover	June – September
Dogs	Welcome between 1st October and 30th April, must be kept on a lead at all times
Useful Websites	www.visit-sunrisecoast.co.uk

Southwold

NEAREST TOWN SOUTHWOLD

Southwold is a family-oriented town with two very different beaches – the Pier Beach and The Denes. It has an almost ironically rejuvenated pier (with art-installation style amusements), chip shops, invariably with long queues, brightly painted houses, many with ship's figureheads above their doors and gracious Georgian villas. At the southern end of the town, between the salt marshes and sand dunes, there's a working harbour with fishing boats and black weatherboarded huts along the edge of the River Blyth opposite Walberswick. A small ferry takes boatloads of people between the two towns throughout summer (the crabbing is better on the Walberswick side). A small caravan and camping site nearby has easy access to The Denes, one of the loveliest beaches in Suffolk – a quiet, dune-backed beach where the water is safe for swimming, canoeing and body-boarding.

The northerly Pier Beach, a mile or so back towards the town and around the corner from the working lighthouse is of Blue Flag standard. It has a high promenade to keep the pounding waves at bay, and is lined with bright and sassily named beach huts. The sands there are groyned but, if you're careful, just as good for swimming. The Latitude Festival, encompassing music, theatre, comedy and film, is held in July in nearby Henham Park.

Cromer

NEAREST TOWN CROMER

It is a sign of the gentrification of north Norfolk that Cromer, once a bright, trashy seaside town, with lots of amusement arcades, kiss-me-quick hats and saucy postcards, is now a quiet spot filled with shops selling scented candles and local art. There's a thriving delicatessen, the pier café sells *paninis* and, while the local crabs are still a big part of the town's economy, they are more likely to be served in a local restaurant than eaten at a street stall.

The sandy and shingle beach is long, not too wide and broken by groynes. There's a cliff-top walk past some Georgian houses up to the working lighthouse, and a huge promenade along the other length of the beach. The pier is usually busy, and the theatre at its end hosts popular summer and Christmas variety shows. There's also a growing surf culture in Cromer and further along the coast westwards to Runton, and a webcam has been installed beside the pier to show the quality of the surf – so you can get there fast when big waves come in.

INFORMATION

Beach Type	Sand and shingle
Facilities	Toilets (including disabled facilities and baby changing), first aid post, cafés and restaurants, shops and a slipway
Activities	RNLI museum (01263 511294) and a theatre on the pier, amusements, Cromer Museum (01263 513543) children's fun area and a surf school (East Coast Surf: 07887 605789)
Parking	Disabled parking along the front only, other car parks available in the town
Information	Cromer Tourist Information Centre (01263 512497)
Lifeguard Cover	June to September
Dogs	Restricted access during the summer, welcome throughout the winter
Useful Websites	www.visitnorfolk.com

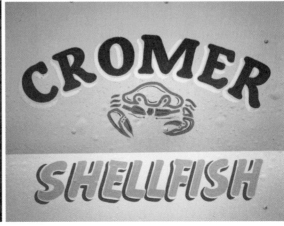

INFORMATION

Beach Type	Sand and shingle
Facilities	Toilets (with disabled facilities), cafés, shower, first aid point and beach huts available for hire (01263 513811)
Activities	Amusement arcade, surfing and other watersports permitted. The North Norfolk Steam Railway is nearby (01263 820800)
Parking	Free on-street parking and parking close to the beach available. No disabled parking spaces
Information	Sheringham Tourist Information Centre (01263 824329)
Lifeguard Cover	19th May to 23rd September
Dogs	Restrictions apply between May and September
Useful Websites	www.norfolkbroads.com www.norfolktouristinformation.com

Sheringham
NEAREST TOWN SHERINGHAM

About 3 miles (5km) along the Norfolk coastal path from Cromer sits the genteel town of Sheringham. Historically, the 'upper' inland part was for agricultural workers, while the 'lower' part near the sea was for fishing families. But for a good few years, Sheringham has been the retirement town of choice for locals who want to be by the sea. There's a working steam railway that runs inland to the market town of Holt, but if the weather's sunny there's little reason why you'd want to stray far from Sheringham's fine beach. It's an unusual combination of shingle and sand: above the high-tide line there's a hill of grey pebbles, but when the tide goes out there's a huge expanse of flat wet sand – perfect for making sand sculptures and drip castles. There are groynes to keep the sand in place, but the swimming is safe. Sheringham is a good base from which to walk the Norfolk Coast Path along the shingle beach and cliffs to Weybourne, Cley and beyond. The old-fashioned family hotels, small pier, open market on Saturdays and absence of large, chain supermarkets (due to local objections), all make Sheringham a very appealing place.

Wells-next-the-Sea

NEAREST TOWN WELLS-NEXT-THE-SEA

Fifty years ago the town thrived on whelk fishing: almost all of England's whelks came into Wells, brought in by the tiny fishing fleet from deep pots far out at sea. Today it's a popular summer holiday destination, with children crabbing off the little wharf on the seafront when the tide is in. The town itself is quaint, with an old granary jutting out into the main street, flint cottages, Georgian houses and a mixture of old-fashioned haberdashery and tool shops together with modern galleries, gift stores and cafés. The beach is rather hidden, about a mile away. Follow the path and road alongside a huge sea wall that runs at right angles to the buildings on the left of the town front. Eventually you'll come to a car park and a line of pine trees. A walk through the trees brings you to the lovely golden sands of this vast beach. A short line of well-kept beach huts on stilts hugs the tree line and looks out to the sea, which can retreat up to a mile at low tide. There are plenty of shells and sea life to be found in the wet sand, and often small lagoons are left behind by the tide on its way out. Beware the quickly returning waters, though; they come in fast.

INFORMATION

Beach Type	Sand
Facilities	Toilets (with disabled facilities in car park), public shower, café/restaurants, first aid post, a variety of shops (along Staithe Street) and camp site (Pinewoods: 01328 710439). Five beach huts are available for hire (through Pinewoods). Additional facilities are available a short walk away in the town
Activities	Sailing, windsurfing and waterskiing available, visit www.wells-guide.co.uk for further listings
Parking	Pay parking (with some disabled access)
Information	Wells Tourist Information Centre (01328 710885)
Lifeguard Cover	A beach warden is on duty from May until the end of September. A siren is sounded when the tide is coming in and there is danger of being trapped on the wrong side of the channel
Dogs	Restrictions apply between May and September
Useful Websites	www.wells-guide.co.uk www.wellsnorfolk.com

Beach Type	Sand
Facilities	None, the closest facilities are about one mile away on the Estate (see Useful Websites for details)
Activities	No organised activities
Parking	Pay parking (with disabled access)
Information	Holkham Estate (01328 710227)
Lifeguard Cover	None
Dogs	Welcome all year, must be kept on lead in certain areas
Useful Websites	www.holkham.co.uk

Holkham

NEAREST TOWN WELLS-NEXT-THE-SEA

The mile-long approach to the entrance of Holkham Beach is possibly one of the grandest in the UK. Turning from the main road (opposite the Victoria Hotel) into Lady Anne's Drive, you can almost imagine that you're heading for a stately home. Instead, after parking and taking the raised walkway through pine trees and dunes, you come out on to a lovely, wide, light golden sandy expanse of beach. When the tide has receded the sea is almost invisible from the dunes, and a walk to the waves can take you through isolated sea puddles, little streams and lots of embedded shells. It's a great place for kite flying, horse riding, beach games or a long peaceful walk. Turning right from the entrance, it's 2 miles (3km) to Wells-next-the-Sea, while a left turn takes you along miles of gorgeous sand towards Burnham Overy Staithe. There's also an easy walkway through the pine trees for a mile or so to a bird hide – the area is a nature reserve and boasts a wealth of rare birds. Looking inland, you can see a monument rising out of the grounds of the Palladian mansion, Holkham Hall. Holkham is a large estate and major employer in the region and, while the owners (Viscount Coke, his wife and four children) live there, it's also open to the public from June to October.

north west

England's north-west coast is one of extreme contrasts: there are miles of quiet, unspoilt beaches north of Barrow-in-Furness; the brash holiday playgrounds of Blackpool and Southport further south; and the industrial docks and shipyards of Liverpool and Ellesmere Port in the Wirral. Two huge estuaries – the Solway Firth and Morecambe Bay – push deep into the coastline, and both have fierce tides running so swiftly that, as Sir Walter Scott wrote: 'well-mounted horsemen lay aside hopes of safety if they see its white surge advancing'.

Roman-built Hadrian's Wall ends at the northern point of Bowness-on-Solway, from where the coastline curves protectively around the high inland peaks of the Lake District National Park. By contrast, low grassy cliffs border the mostly sandy beaches, which are broken by 'scars', large areas of rock and shingle offshore. The highest point on this stretch of coastline is the red sandstone cliffs of St. Bees, over 300ft (91m) high, with wonderful views (and sunsets) across the Irish Sea to the Isle of Man.

CUMBRIA

St. Bees •

Seascale •

• Lytham St. Anne

• Ainsdale

Formby •

Wallasey •

Further down the coast, past the 150 square miles (38 hectares) of mud flats and quicksands of Morecambe Bay, are the sandy beaches of Blackpool and the classic family seaside town of neighbouring Lytham St. Annes. From Southport to Liverpool, the coastal plain is unremittingly flat and the River Mersey shoreline is dotted with docklands, steelworks and shipbuilders – yet there are still tranquil spots such as Ainsdale and Formby, both of which have beautiful beaches and nature reserves where you can encounter rare wildlife including native red squirrels and natterjack toads. Despite the area's industrial heritage, there are still long, sandy beaches on the Mersey and sea coasts of the Wirral: from New Brighton and Wallasey beach, you can watch the commercial ships from Liverpool docks go by and marvel at the proud industrial and maritime traditions of this once-mighty port.

CASHIRE

Wallasey

NEAREST TOWN WALLASEY VILLAGE

Also known as New Brighton beach, this mile-long stretch of flat, golden sand offers unobstructed views across the Mersey to Liverpool, and if you walk westward around the headland you find a long, wide stretch of sand that borders the North Wirral coastal park. The beach was extremely popular in and around the mid-20th century, and it's still an excellent place for a family day out and to watch the boats go by. There's a long marine promenade and high sea wall, a lighthouse and a 19th-century fort and museum, Perch Rock, originally cut off at high tide, but which can now be approached by a raised roadway – on a hot, sunny day, it looks almost like a Saharan fortress rising from the sands. Along the sea front there are some impressive Art Deco buildings and many attractions, including a bowling alley, amusement arcade, funfair, model boating lake and the Floral Pavilion Theatre. Unfortunately, the open-air sea-water swimming pool was destroyed by bad weather in 1990, but you can swim in the sea (although the undercurrents are strong here, so stay within designated markers). Renowned photographer Martin Parr has captured many memorable images of Wallasey beach in his book, *The Last Resort*.

Beach Type	Sand
Facilities	Toilets (with disabled facilities), lifeguard and first aid post, slipway to the beach and a local pub
Activities	Adjacent to the beach is a pitch and putt course at the Wallasey Golf Club (0151 6911024) and the Floral Pavilion Theatre (0151 6660000)
Parking	Free parking available
Information	Wirral Ranger Service (0151 6785488)
Lifeguard Cover	March to September
Dogs	Welcome all year
Useful Websites	www.wirral.gov.uk www.wallaseygolfclub.com

INFORMATION

Beach Type	Sand
Facilities	Toilets (with disabled facilities and baby changing). They close at 5.30pm in summer and 4pm in winter. Shop and amenities in the village
Activities	No organised activities
Parking	Pay parking available. Car park closes at 5.30pm April to October and 4pm November to March
Information	Liverpool Tourist Information Centre (0151 7070986) or National Trust Office (01704 878591)
Lifeguard Cover	None
Dogs	Welcome, but must be kept on leads
Useful Websites	www.nationaltrust.org.uk

Formby

NEAREST TOWN SOUTHPORT

The beach at Formby is about a mile from the village itself, the two separated by high dunes known locally as the Formby Hills. From the highest of the hills, with binoculars, it is possible to see the clock on the Liver building 11 miles (18km) south, so flat is the west Lancashire coastal plain between Liverpool and Formby (in fact some of this area is below sea level). Formby is a completely unspoilt, wild and wide sandy beach, and although it gets busy with day trippers from Liverpool and the north-west in summer, the rest of the year it's a quiet and peaceful spot.

The National Trust has run the beach since 1967 and much of the land around is a Special Area of Conservation. There are miles of walks through the pine forests and a red squirrel reserve – you might catch sight of a drey or nest in the trees (sadly, the numbers of squirrels are diminishing because of a virulent outbreak of squirrel pox). Rabbits and foxes are also common. In spring around the dunes, marram grass and pools, the male natterjack toads (pictured right) sing their mating song – known locally as the 'Bootle organ' – to attract mates. The village is quiet, and has been home to a number of professional football players from nearby Liverpool and Everton clubs in recent years. Its shopping facilities and the presence of numerous golf clubs reflect the wealth of the area.

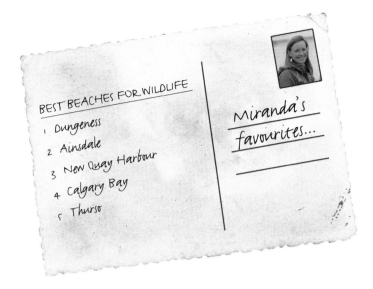

BEST BEACHES FOR WILDLIFE

1 Dungeness
2 Ainsdale
3 New Quay Harbour
4 Calgary Bay
5 Thurso

Miranda's favourites...

Ainsdale

NEAREST TOWN SOUTHPORT

South of the Ribble estuary and below Southport, with the oldest iron-built pier in Britain, sits the sandy, dune-backed beach of Ainsdale. Considered to be the main bathing beach of Southport, it is long and flat, and the sand is so compact that well into the 1970s people were allowed to drive along the beach to Southport (speed limit 10mph). These days you're far more likely to spot a kite buggy on the sand than a Ford Escort – this is only local beach where land-based traction kiting is allowed. The low tides and vast expanse of sand make this a popular spot for beach sports of all kinds. The dunes behind form one of the most important conservation areas in the north west – a National Nature Reserve and home to more than 450 wild plant species including dune helleborine, seaside centaury and yellow bartsia, and wildlife such as great-crested newts, sand lizards and natterjack toads. Behind the dunes is a pine forest where you can spot native red squirrels, and a short walk away is the village of Ainsdale, with its boating lake and varied shopping and eating places. Ainsdale is also on the Sefton Coastal Path, which stretches for 12 miles (19km) between Southport and Crosby, where Liverpool meets the sea.

INFORMATION

Beach Type	Sand
Facilities	Toilets (with disabled facilities), cafés, first aid post and lost child services available with the lifeguard
Activities	Many activities – including windsurfing and guided walks – are available from the Discovery Centre (0151 9342967). The Natural England Nature Reserve (01704 578774) offers further walks in the area
Parking Information	Pay parking available during summer season Southport Tourist Information Centre (01704 533333)
Lifeguard Cover	Easter to September
Dogs	Dogs are banned 218yd (200m) either side of the main beach entrance down to the tide line
Useful websites	www.visitsouthport.com

Lytham St. Annes

NEAREST TOWN LYTHAM ST. ANNES

Next door to Blackpool, west of Preston and extremely genteel, the seaside resort of Lytham St. Annes could be a thousand miles from the one-armed bandits of Blackpool's Golden Mile. A sandy beach and promenade runs around the coast between the originally separate towns of St. Annes (to the north) and Lytham. This is a classic family seaside destination, with donkey rides on the sand, a renovated Victorian pier, children's playgrounds, Lytham's famous green windmill, cafés, ice-cream parlours and municipal gardens. It's a place of irresistible, old-fashioned charm. At the Lytham end, there's the Ribble estuary, where the sand turns to mud. This makes the area unsuitable for swimming but great for bird-watching – more than 250,000 waders and wildfowl including widgeons, dunlins, sanderlings and godwits visit each year. At Fairhaven Lake beside the beach (where there's putting, bowling, tennis and boating), there's an interactive RSPB Discovery Centre, where you can learn all about the wildlife in the estuary. The town is also internationally renowned for the Royal Lytham & St. Annes golf course, host to British Open Golf Championships and numerous other major tournaments.

Beach Type	Sand	
Facilities	Toilets, a variety of shops and cafés, pubs and restaurants	
Activities	There is a Nature Reserve (01253 725610), donkey rides during the summer season, amusement park and a golf course next to the beach	
Parking	Pay parking (with disabled access) and roadside parking available	
Information	Blackpool Tourist Information Centre (01253 621623)	
Lifeguard Cover	None	
Dogs	Restrictions apply between May and September. Details are clearly flagged on the beach.	
Useful Websites	www.visitlythamstannes.co.uk	

Beach Type	Sand and shingle
Facilities	Toilets (with disabled facilities) and a wooden jetty
Activities	No organised activities. The Sellafield Centre (01946 727027) is open to visitors Monday to Friday during working hours
Parking	Free parking (with disabled access) available
Information	Egremont Tourist Information Centre (01946 820693)
Lifeguard Cover	None
Dogs	Welcome all year
Useful Websites	www.visitegremont.com www.visitcumbria.com

Seascale

NEAREST TOWN EGREMONT

Lying in the shadow of the chimneys of Sellafield nuclear plant, the town of Seascale stretches along the top of low-lying cliffs. Below, there's a boulder-strewn beach and at low tide, the sands stretch away to the horizon, with views over the Irish Sea to the Isle of Man and beyond. It's an idyllic spot, one of the most tranquil beaches in the north west of England. The village was a popular resort in Victorian times when the newly built Furness railway brought holidaymakers from the cities. Today, a railway line still runs alongside the beach, which has a wooden jetty, a listed water tower and children's playground on the sea front. The village is thought to date back to Norse times, and there is evidence of older settlements in the area. In a farmer's field just to the south of Sellafield stand the ten stones of Grey Croft stone circle, where many Bronze Age artefacts have been found. There are lovely walks on the beach and countryside around Seascale – in local shops you can buy a parish council booklet showing the best of them. The Sellafield Centre is open to visitors, and runs various educational programmes and exhibitions throughout the year.

St. Bees

NEAREST TOWN ST. BEES

Situated at the most westerly point of Cumbria, the small village of St. Bees is beautifully positioned at the end of a valley, just south of Whitehaven, with a long sandy beach beginning near St. Bees Head. Legend has it that the village was named after a 7th-century Irish princess, St. Bega, who landed here after escaping an enforced marriage and founded a nunnery (since destroyed). There's also a 16th-century school called St. Bees, built by Edmund Grindal, a local boy who became Archbishop of Canterbury.

Despite its considerable history, it's the natural beauty of the place that really impresses. The red sandstone cliffs of the head are over 300ft (91m) high and a haven for nesting seabirds such as puffins, razorbills, terns and black guillemots. On a clear day, you can see from here to the Isle of Man and north to Scotland. The beach at St. Bees is a natural bay backed by low cliffs and shingle that runs into a wide expanse of golden sand when the tide is out. Wooden groynes near the village protect against coastal erosion and, as long as you avoid these, the sea is fine for swimming in good weather. You'll often see paragliders launching from the low cliffs, and you can walk along these as part of the Cumbria Coastal Way. St. Bees is also the starting point of Alfred Wainwright's famous 1972 Coast to Coast walk across England – it's 190 miles (305km) from St. Bees Head to Robin Hood's Bay in north Yorkshire across what he called 'the grandest territory in northern England'.

INFORMATION

Beach Type	Sand and shingle
Facilities	Toilets, camp sites close by, promenade, café and a slipway. The village also provides a range of services
Activities	There is a children's playground on the main beach
Parking	Pay parking available
Information	Egremont Tourist Information Centre (01946 820693)
Lifeguard Cover	None
Dogs	Welcome, but please be responsible
Useful Websites	www.stbees.org.uk

north east

Some of England's finest beaches and most stunning natural scenery are on the north-east coast, but because of the area's industrial heritage these have often been neglected. No longer – even the once-polluted Durham coastline between the Rivers Tyne and Tees has now been cleaned up and transformed into the Durham Heritage Coast, a nature conservation area, with restored limestone grasslands and cliff environments, and a wonderful area for walking. Today the varied north-east coastline stretching from the muddy shallows of the Wash to the majestic cliffs, deserted white sands and ruined castles of Northumberland, is well worth visiting.

Despite its flat landscape, the Lincolnshire coastline provides miles and miles of beautiful, often isolated, golden sands with enduring holiday resorts such as Skegness, Mablethorpe and Sutton-on-Sea dotted along its strands. Heading north, over the Humber, you'll find the spectacular scenery and great swimming beaches of the Yorkshire coast.

NORTH

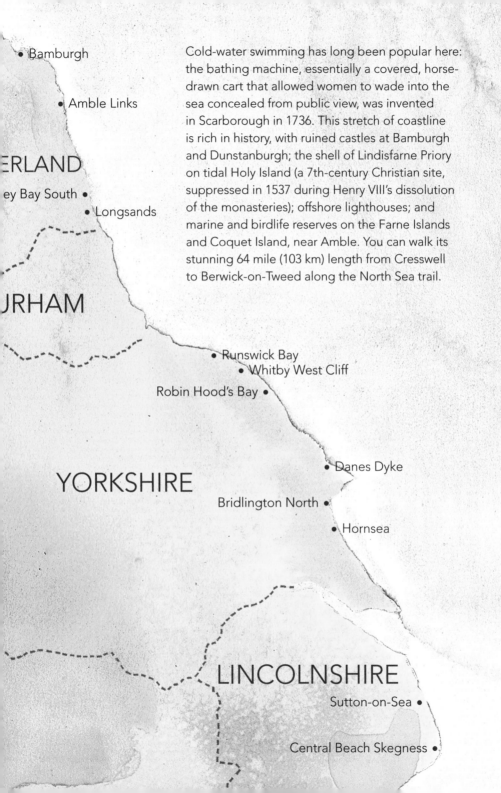

Bamburgh

Amble Links

ERLAND

ey Bay South

Longsands

JRHAM

Cold-water swimming has long been popular here:
the bathing machine, essentially a covered, horse-
drawn cart that allowed women to wade into the
sea concealed from public view, was invented
in Scarborough in 1736. This stretch of coastline
is rich in history, with ruined castles at Bamburgh
and Dunstanburgh; the shell of Lindisfarne Priory
on tidal Holy Island (a 7th-century Christian site,
suppressed in 1537 during Henry VIII's dissolution
of the monasteries); offshore lighthouses; and
marine and birdlife reserves on the Farne Islands
and Coquet Island, near Amble. You can walk its
stunning 64 mile (103 km) length from Cresswell
to Berwick-on-Tweed along the North Sea trail.

Runswick Bay

Whitby West Cliff

Robin Hood's Bay

Danes Dyke

YORKSHIRE

Bridlington North

Hornsea

LINCOLNSHIRE

Sutton-on-Sea

Central Beach Skegness

JoLLY SKEGY (handwritten)

Central Beach Skegness

NEAREST TOWN SKEGNESS

South from Sutton-on-Sea at the top of the north side of The Wash, and with 6 miles (9.5km) of golden sands, Skegness is something of a neglected gem. Voted best place to retire in a 2005 magazine poll, the town was founded in the mid-19th century when a railway line was built from the industrial Midlands to the coast, bringing with it hordes of holidaying factory workers. In its prime, the town had more than 100,000 flowering plants along its promenade, a fine, mile-long (1.6km) artificial waterway and a pier a third of a mile long (0.4km). Sadly, the pier was truncated by a fire in the 1980s, and only the land-based end, which houses amusements, remains. But there are lots more traditional entertainments to be found, including donkey rides on the wide golden sands of the beach in summer. Swimming is good and when it's windy and the tide is high, there's great surfing and body-boarding, too. And the views are peerless; on a clear day you can see across The Wash to the north Norfolk coast. In many ways this is the perfect old-fashioned English seaside experience.

WAS 8 y o A WOW (handwritten)

INFORMATION	**Beach Type**	Sand
	Facilities	Toilets (with disabled facilities and baby changing), first aid post, slip way and a variety of cafés, restaurants and other food options close to the beach
	Activities	Activities run during the school holidays, see Useful Websites for further details, donkey rides run during the summer
	Parking	Pay parking available
	Information	Skegness Tourist Information Centre (01754 899887)
	Lifeguard Cover	June to September
	Dogs	Restrictions apply from May to September
	Useful Websites	www.funcoast.co.uk

INFORMATION	**Beach Type**	Sand
	Facilities	Toilets (with disabled facilities), cafés, restaurants and a first aid post
	Activities	Pleasure Gardens which include a paddling pool, tennis, crazy golf, bowls and tearooms. A promenade, beach furniture and huts are available for hire (01754 897435)
	Parking	Pay parking available
	Information	Sutton-on-Sea Tourist Information Centre (01507 441373)
	Lifeguard Cover	June to September
	Dogs	Not permitted between 1st May and 30th September on the Main Beach
	Useful Websites	www.suttononsea.info www.visitlincolnshire.co.uk

Sutton-on-Sea

NEAREST TOWN MABLETHORPE

The coastline of Lincolnshire is flat and wide, the sky seemingly bigger than anywhere else in Britain, and it's possible to walk along the 6 mile (9.5km) beach from Saltfleet south to Sutton-on-Sea and not see more than a handful of people along the way.

Sutton, set beside the bigger, better-known resort of Mablethorpe, is a bit of a hidden secret. It's a traditional, old-fashioned seaside town with wide, clean, golden sands that are perfect for playing beach rounders, picnicking, making sandcastles and catching flatfish (pictured right), crabs and shrimps. The beach is rarely crowded and has such spectacular sea views that time passes unnoticed just watching the waves roll in. Swimming is safe, as long as you avoid the groynes. The beach huts on the front of the promenade are eclectic and colourful – you can hire some of them by the day. Most are privately owned and extremely well kept as befits a town that holds the country's only Bathing Beauties Festival (including a Beautiful Beach Hut competition) every September – a weekend of music, arts, poetry and song that culminates in a huge firework display on the beach.

Hornsea

NEAREST TOWN HORNSEA

The lovely, wide, sandy beach at Hornsea has been the victim of longshore drift for centuries. At the turn of the 20th century, proper sea defences were built, including a high sea wall in front of the redbrick houses at the edge of town. Today there are a further line of boulders in front of the wall, groynes and a steel gabion to protect the caravan park above the beach to the south. The pull of the sea does wonders for the quality of driftwood on the beach – you will find some beautifully smooth specimens. And don't worry about the brown sea water, it's just sediment raised by the tide; the water quality is high.

When it's sunny, there's nothing to beat Hornsea beach for a good family day out. The seafront is cheap and cheerful, there's a leisure centre with a swimming pool, and you can get locally caught fish in the many chip shops near the award-winning promenade. Just inland sits Hornsea Mere, the largest freshwater lake in the north east and an RSPB reserve, so home to many wildfowl and birds. You can also sail, row and fish on the lake.

Beach Type	Sand and shingle
Facilities	Toilets (with disabled facilities), café and restaurants, shops, first aid post, promenade, slip way, leisure centre, beach huts available for hire (01964 566333)
Activities	No organised activities
Parking	Pay parking and some free street parking
Information	Bridlington Tourist Information Centre (01262 673474) or the Foreshore Office (01262 678255)
Lifeguard Cover	This is decided on a seasonal basis, contact the Foreshore Office (01262 678255)
Dogs	Not welcome from May to September
Useful Websites	www.realyorkshire.co.uk

INFORMATION

Beach Type	Sand
Facilities	Toilets (with disabled facilities), beach huts and deck chairs available for hire (details along the seafront), information point, first aid post and lost child centre, a variety of cafés and food outlets available
Activities	The Land Train operates from Leisure World via Limekiln Lane to Sewerby Hall. Leisure World (01262 606715) offers a range of activities.Donkey rides are available during the summer season
Parking	Pay parking (with disabled access)
Information	Bridlington Tourist Information Centre (01262 673474) or the Foreshore Office (01262 678255)
Lifeguard Cover	July to August
Dogs	Restrictions apply between May and September
Useful Websites	www.realyorkshire.co.uk

Bridlington

NEAREST TOWN BRIDLINGTON

With its spa waters and elegant, Georgian houses, Bridlington is a perfect example of a well-kept northern seaside town. It has two piers, with fine sandy beaches stretching away in both directions as far as the eye can see. Near the piers there are many groynes and the sand is kept spotlessly clean by the local council. The promenades are flanked with pretty beach huts.

Bridlington was established as a resort, thanks to the health-giving chalybeate spring discovered in the early 19th century (prompting the construction of the Royal Spa Hotel). The old town dates back to pre-Roman times and has some fine priory ruins. The sea front has been built around the quay between the piers, which has always provided good mooring for sail boats and large ships – such as the one which landed Queen Henrietta Maria in 1643 on her quest to help her husband Charles I in the Civil War. Because Bridlington sits below the 7 mile (11km) long chalk promontory of Flamborough Head, it is protected from strong north-easterly winds and has avoided much of the coastal erosion that so plagues the rest of the region.

This is a traditional family resort, with beaches that have been declared among the best for making sandcastles, and with lots of attractions. These include the Land Train (which takes passengers around the town), the Bridlington Eye (a smaller version of the London Eye), the Harbour Museum and a Beside The Seaside Experience Museum (full of exhibits and waxwork scenes from the town's past).

Danes Dyke

NEAREST TOWN BRIDLINGTON ✓

Running north to south across Flamborough Head, this Iron Age ditch and flat-topped bank earthwork forms the border of one of the country's finest and most important nature reserves. There's a beach at the southern end of the Dyke, just below a good viewing point to Bridlington Bay, and a fabulous coastal walk around the headland (coming back inland) on the 1¾ mile (3km) circular Tree Trail. As well as protected seabird colonies, you will also catch sight of many unusual land birds during autumn migration and over-wintering from Scandinavia. There's a bridle path where you can ride horses (you can hire them nearby), and a beacon light tower, which is the only known example in England, built in 1674. The beach itself is stony and naturally chalky, about three-quarters of a mile (1.2km) long, and offers a treasure chest of fossils for hunters – although it's recommended that children stay away from the cliffs because of falling rocks. Getting on to the beach is easy as there's a car park with toilet facilities just above the entrance to the Dyke. However, it's well worth checking tide tables before setting out, because high tide comes up to the cliffs.

✓ YES

INFORMATION

Beach Type	Sand and pebble
Facilities	Toilets, café at the car park and a slipway
Activities	No organised activities, although the fossils are good
Parking	Pay parking (with disabled access) available
Information	Bridlington Tourist Information Centre (01262 673474)
Lifeguard Cover	None
Dogs	Welcome all year
Useful Websites	www.realyorkshire.co.uk

Robin Hood's Bay

NEAREST TOWN WHITBY

Yes it's a long way from Nottingham and, no, Robin Hood didn't retire to this lovely, higgledy-piggledy former fishing village that wends its way down a steep hill to the sea. Folklore has it that the robber of the rich kept a boat in the bay to escape from the clutches of the law, but the main historical relevance of the area dates back much further than Robin Hood – for this is the Dinosaur Coast. The beaches and cliffs are full of ammonites, belemnites, reptilian and dinosaur fossils and footprints from Jurassic and Cretaceous eras. You'll see many fossils on the rocks and along the bottom of the honeycombed, sedimentary cliffs that run 5 miles (8km) north to Whitby and a couple of miles south to Boggle Hole (a pebbly cove at the mouth of a stream). The road down into the old village ends at the sea in a concrete wedge of land that is lapped by the high tide. But at low tide you'll find a small sandy beach, also approachable from a path on the cliff top. Gorgeous walks, a cycle path, horseriding for all abilities and many excellent tearooms make Robin Hood's Bay a very good day out.

Beach Type	Sand and rock
Facilities	Toilets (with disabled facilities), thriving village with good facilities nearby
Activities	There's so much to do in this area, see websites listed below for information on all events and listings
Parking	There are two car parks, one at the top of the bay (with disabled access) and one at the top of the hill
Information	Whitby Tourist Information Centre (01723 383636)
Lifeguard Cover	None
Dogs	Welcome all year round
Useful Websites	www.robin-hoods-bay.co.uk www.discoveryorkshirecoast.com

Beach Type	Sand
Facilities	Toilets (with disabled facilities), first aid post, lost child centre, café/restaurants, beach huts available for hire (01947 602124) and a slipway
Activities	No organised activities
Parking	Both free and pay parking available close to the beach
Information	Whitby Tourist Information (01723 383636)
Lifeguard Cover	June to September
Dogs	Banned from 1st May to 30th September
Useful Websites	www.blueflag.org www.discoveryorkshirecoast.com

Whitby West Cliff

FANTASTIC VIEWS

NEAREST TOWN WHITBY *STILL QUAINT*

There's a great deal of history in Whitby, including connections with whaling, and the explorer Captain James Cook was born nearby and lived in the town. Bram Stoker stayed in the town and his novel *Dracula* was famously inspired by the craggy cliffs, wild seas and narrow lanes running inland uphill (built for workers in the 18th century to get to the shore to land the tonnes of whale blubber that came through the town). A whale-bone arch, situated close to Cook's bronze statue on the West Cliff, commemorates the whaling industry. Whitby was also home of the man who 'invented' the crow's nest lookout on sail ships, Captain William Scoresby.

When the whaling and fishing died and tourists began to visit the town in the late 19th century, the golden sands of West Cliff became the focal point of the attractions. The beach runs to the aptly named Sandsend, where you can find the Wit's End café, famous for its home-made cakes. There are several shallow-laying shipwrecks off the coast for divers to explore, lots of traditional amusements, including a summer theatre, and a museum close to the majestic ruins of Whitby Abbey on the cliff top. The East Cliff stands above a very rocky coast full of fossils (check the tides before venturing down the cliff as incoming tides can be dangerous). There is one of the most highly regarded fish and chips shops in the country here; the Magpie café. Go early, as queues can be long.

Runswick Bay

NEAREST TOWN WHITBY

Seated at the edge of the North Yorkshire Moors National Park, Runswick offers a rare and welcome stretch of sand on what is otherwise a walker's coast. Because it is sheltered by the lofty crag of Lingrow Knowle, the bay is a tranquil spot where you can moor a boat, or simply pitch a deck chair and take a swim – it's one of the few safe swimming areas for quite a few miles (although be careful when there are strong north-easterly winds). Quaint red-roofed houses nestle into the hillside at the north of the bay, but in the early part of the 17th century the whole village (bar one house) slid into the sea. In 1970, a new sea wall was built to ensure the village's safety from erosion and today Runswick is a haven for artists and wildlife lovers. While it comes to life in the summer months as a holiday destination, it offers peace and tranquillity in winter. Be aware of the ramp down to the beach and car park, which is a 1-in-4 gradient. At low tide the mile-long (1.6km) beach reveals rocky outcrops and stones which hold countless fossils. It is a great place for beachcombing. You might also see a few fishing boats dashing up and down the coast, the remnants of what was once the dominant industry in the area.

Beach Type	Sand and rock
Facilities	Toilets available
Activities	Sailing and waterskiing (both at Runswick Bay Beach and Sailing Club: www.rbbsc.co.uk)
Parking	Pay and Display in the lower village
Information	Whitby Tourist Information Centre (01723 383636)
Lifeguard Cover	None
Dogs	Welcome all year
Useful Websites	www.runswick.com www.discoveryorkshirecoast.com

Longsands ✓

NEAREST TOWN TYNEMOUTH ✓   ℕICÉ

S teep grassy slopes at the edge of Tynemouth's suburban sprawl look down over the sweeping curve of Longsands beach. Actually the sands aren't that long – the beach stretches for only about half a mile (0.8km), although the sand is golden and the swimming good. At the far end, sitting at the foot of sloping grass banks, you'll find an extraordinary man-made, sea-water swimming pool. Built in 1925 and in use for more than 70 years, it's now a derelict rock pool but you can imagine the swimming galas and grand social events that were once held here. Longsands is now a popular surfing spot with locals, especially after a storm and strong northerly winds, and has hosted the British Cup, the national surfing championships. There's also the Blue Reef Aquarium on Grand Parade, where you can see giant octopuses, sharks, seahorses, seals and other aquatic wildlife.

If Longsands gets too busy, walk south to King Edward's Bay, which is overlooked by the ruins of 11th-century Tynemouth Priory and Castle. The bay, sheltered between rock formations, is sandy and swimming is safe if the weather's not too rough. You can visit the Priory and Castle (managed by English Heritage), nearby Watch House to see relics of shipwrecks, or take a walk along the cliffs for the fantastic views of the shipping that continues in the Tyne.

INFORMATION

Beach Type	Sand
Facilities	Toilets (with disabled facilities), first aid post, lost child centre, café/restaurants and shops
Activities	Surf board hire available (Tynemouth Surf Company: 0191 2582496), windsurfing, sea canoeing, scuba diving, snorkelling permitted, with zoning for watersports. The Blue Reef Aquarium (0191 2581031) is close by
Parking	Pay parking (including disabled access) available
Information	Whitley Bay Tourist Information Centre (0191 2008535)
Lifeguard Cover	May to September
Dogs	Not permitted from 1st May to 30th September
Useful Websites	www.longsandsbeach.co.uk www.visitnewcastlegateshead.co.uk

INFORMATION

Beach Type	Sand and rock
Facilities	Toilets (with disabled facilities), cafés, restaurants, bars and a promenade
Activities	Sea kayaking, surfing and mini golf. There are various watersports companies in the local area. St. Mary's Lighthouse Visitor Centre nearby (0191 2008650)
Parking	Pay and display parking (with disabled access) available
Information	Whitley Bay Tourist Information Centre (0191 2008535)
Lifeguard Cover	May to September
Dogs	Dog exercise area provided, restricted elsewhere between May and September
Useful Websites	www.whitleybaysite.info www.northumberland-coast.co.uk

Whitley Bay South

NEAREST TOWN WHITLEY BAY

Don't be put off by the memory of the once-great industrial might of this area. Where huge tankers used to steam into the mouth of the Tyne day and night, it is now mostly peaceful. The town of Whitley Bay has an old-fashioned seafront, with its once-famous dome, fairground sites, paddling pools and boating lakes slightly faded and awaiting regeneration. That leaves the wonders of nature to entertain visitors, and they don't disappoint. The beach and seafront to the north of the parade is long and lovely. Walk along the magnificent sands and across the causeway to St. Mary's Island, marked by its gleaming white lighthouse (decommissioned) and former keepers' cottages. The island is now a visitor centre and nature reserve, and you can climb the steps to the top of the lighthouse for views of the coastline, or search among the many rockpools below for crabs and sealife. Dangerous swimming areas are well marked; for the best bathing head south through the town to the small sheltered beach at Cullercoats Bay, a sandy cove between stone piers, with an old Victorian lifeboat house, where the waves are very safe.

Amble Links ✓

NEAREST TOWN AMBLE ✓

The town of Amble spills around a harbour, originally built to export coal, but which now mainly plays host to bird-watchers, coastal walkers and families who enjoy the sand and shingle beach for its rock pools and the sea-life they hold. As well as the beautiful sandy beach, which forms part of Northumberland's stunning Heritage Coast, the town has a marina and fishing harbour. The finest sands are just south of the harbour towards Hauxley, which offers a great view of Coquet Island and its working lighthouse. Situated less than a mile from the coast, the island holds the ruins of a medieval monastery (from which the lighthouse was constructed). It's owned by the Duke of Northumberland whose family live at Alnwick Castle – the Hogwarts of the early Harry Potter films – a few miles north and inland from Amble. The castle and gardens are well worth a visit. Coquet is managed by the RSPCA and it is reckoned to be home to more than 18,000 nesting puffins (pictured right), as well as the largest UK colony of the endangered roseate tern. Although you can't land on the island, there are regular bird-watching cruises from Amble, whatever the weather.

INFORMATION

Beach Type	Sand
Facilities	Toilets (with disabled access) shops, café/restaurant, harbour and marina
Activities	A variety of watersports are available (Coquet Shorebase Trust: 01665 710367)
Parking	Free parking
Information	Amble Tourist Information Centre (01665 712313)
Lifeguard Cover	None
Dogs	Welcome all year
Useful Websites	www.northumberland-beaches.co.uk

FANTASTIC BIRDS

INFORMATION

Beach Type	Sand
Facilities	Toilets (with disabled facilities) located in the castle, café/restaurant
Activities	Surfing, windsurfing, swimming and fishing permitted. Horseriding at Slate Hall Riding Centre, based in Seahouses (01665 720320)
Parking	Pay parking available
Information	Berwick-upon-Tweed Tourist Information Centre (01289 330733)
Lifeguard Cover	None
Dogs	Welcome all year
Useful Websites	www.visitnorthumberland.com www.northumberland-coast.co.uk

Bamburgh

HOO - RAY

NEAREST TOWN SEAHOUSES

Bamburgh beach is the perfect fusion of man and nature. The beach, shelted by dunes, stretches for mile upon mile of magnificent golden sands, and dominating the skyline is the majestic outline of Bamburgh Castle. It's one of England's most dramatic sights: largely restored in Victorian times (when it was used as a school to train servant girls), its sandstone towers and walls drop to the rocks below to form a 164ft (50m) precipice.

Turn right on the beach and you can walk south to Seahouses, 3 miles (5km) away, meandering past the rocky reefs picking up shells and unusual stones and, if you're lucky, catching sight of grey seals or the puffins and guillemots that nest on the outlying Farne Islands. In winter, this is a fantastic spot to look out for rare birds such as long-tailed ducks and grey plovers. To the north above the beach, a path leads up to a lighthouse on the clifftop, and you can see the ghostly shape of Holy Island and Lindisfarne Castle in the distance.

Bamburgh beach is quiet, clean and litter-free, even during the main holiday season, so you can always bag a peaceful spot to lay your towel. It's a great destination for families: swimming is safe, provided that you avoid the rocks (and bad weather), and surfers rate the waves, which break left and right by way of shifting sand bars. The castle is also a tourist hot spot, offering visitors tours around its china, porcelain, furniture, painting and arms collections, from March to October (it's also licensed for weddings). Try the crab sandwiches, caught locally.

Wales

On the north coast of Wales, stretching from Flint
in the River Dee's tidal estuary to the island of
Anglesey, you will find the traditional seaside
and sandy beach towns of Rhyl, Colwyn Bay
and Llandudno, some towering cliffside scenery
and Edward I's magnificent castles at Conway and
Beaumaris. Anglesey itself, the last stronghold of
the Druids (beaten by Roman forces in AD61), has
secluded, unspoilt beaches, backed with rolling
grassy dunes or rugged cliffs, often with distant
views of the mountain peaks of Snowdonia
(pictured right). To the south of Wales's 1,680 mile
(2,703km) coastline is the Llyn peninsula with the
500ft (152m) cliffs of Mynydd Mawr and views to
the island of Bardsey – a Christian place of
pilgrimage since the early Middle Ages (three
trips to Bardsey equalled one to Rome) and now
a National Nature Reserve. There's the wild,
south-west facing, surfing beach of Hell's Mouth,
yet just around the corner is sheltered Abersoch,
with its own microclimate and spectacular views
across Tremadoc Bay to Harlech and down the
long sweep of Cardigan Bay. From the pretty,
colourwashed, fishing towns of Aberaeron and

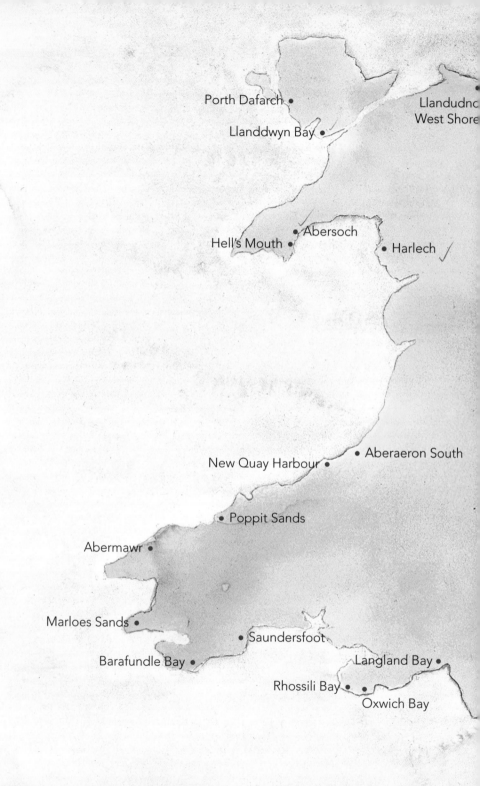

Porth Dafarch •

Llandudno
West Shore

Llanddwyn Bay •

Abersoch
Hell's Mouth •

Harlech ✓

Aberaeron South •

New Quay Harbour •

Poppit Sands •

Abermawr •

Marloes Sands •

Saundersfoot •

Langland Bay •

Barafundle Bay •

Rhossili Bay •

Oxwich Bay

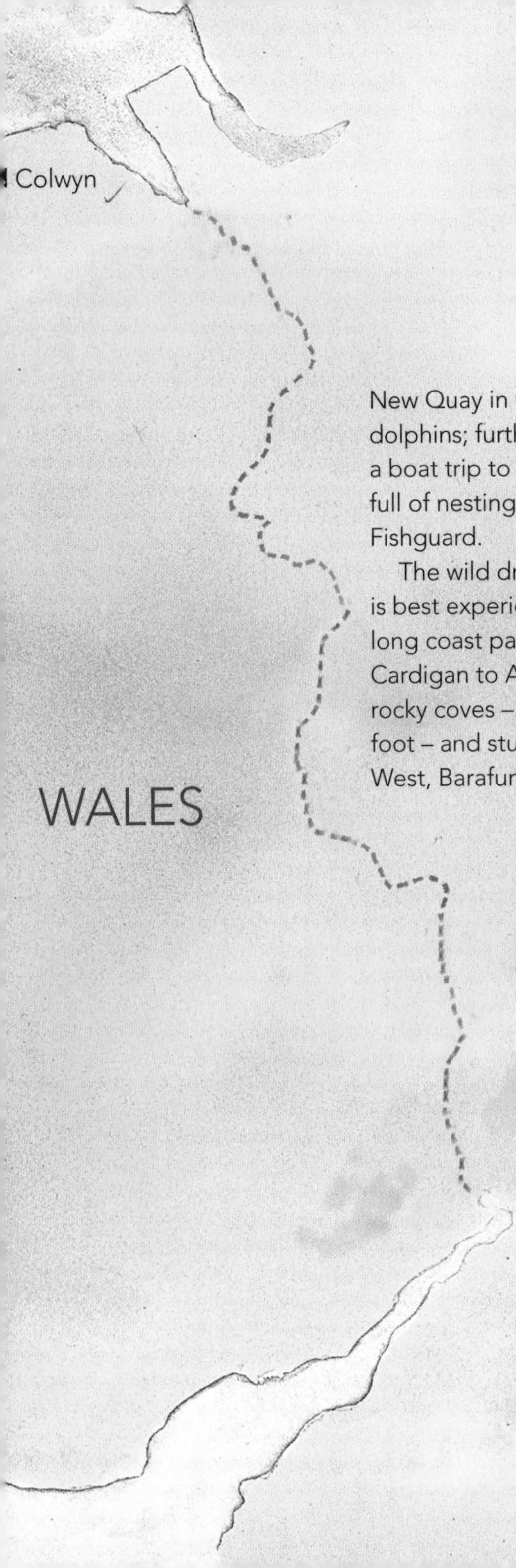

Colwyn

New Quay in Ceredigion you can spot bottlenose
dolphins; further around the coast, you can take
a boat trip to see the caves, coves and black cliffs
full of nesting birds between Poppit Sands and
Fishguard.

The wild drama of the Pembrokeshire coast
is best experienced from the 186 mile (299km)
long coast path that leads you from St. Dogmaels,
Cardigan to Amroth, near Tenby past countless
rocky coves – many of which are accessible only by
foot – and stunning sandy beaches at Freshwater
West, Barafundle Bay and Saundersfoot.

WALES

INFORMATION

Beach Type	Sand with rocky outcrops
Facilities	Toilets (with disabled facilities), lost child centre and a first aid post, plus a variety of shops and cafés. Beach huts are available for hire (01792 635436)
Activities	Tennis courts for hire (01792 363105)
Parking	Pay parking (with disabled access)
Information	Swansea Tourist Information Centre (01792 468321) or the Foreshore Department (01792 636000)
Lifeguard Cover	May to September
Dogs	Banned from May to September
Useful Websites	www.visitswanseabay.com

Langland Bay

NEAREST TOWN SWANSEA

Just around the headland from the pretty Victorian seaside village of Mumbles lie the wide, golden sands and rock pools of Langland Bay. This is an extremely popular bathing and family beach, packed with local families and holidaymakers from nearby Swansea during the summer months. The walk down from the coastal path is steep, and there's a café with spectacular balcony views of the bay. The south-west facing beach is fringed by a row of striped wooden beach huts, and just offshore is the rocky reef of Crab Island. Langland Bay is a big surfing destination especially in winter: there are both left and right breaks onto the beach, and the low-tide right-hand wave over Crab Island is meant to be one of the best surfing experiences in Wales. On the foreshore, there are tennis courts, cafés and other amenities, and lifeguards during the summer season. You can walk around the steep coastal path to the sandy beach of Caswell Bay, about 1½ miles (2.5km) away – from the cliff tops there are wonderful views over the Bristol Channel to the hills of north Devon. Mumbles itself is well worth a visit for the shops, galleries, surfing outlets and restaurants.

Oxwich Bay

NEAREST TOWN SWANSEA

This is one of the Gower's most dramatic and popular beaches, a haven for sailing and other watersports, and a great summer family holiday destination. The beach is busiest at the town end near the slipway where boats are launched – it's best to avoid this area when swimming – and quieter heading eastwards towards the dunes and limestone rocks around Great Tor (highly picturesque). You can walk over 2 miles (3km) along the golden sands of Oxwich Bay to the three rocky pyramids of the aptly named Three Cliffs Bay – at least when the tide is out.

Behind the beach's huge sand dunes are the salt and fresh water marshes and woodlands of Oxwich Burrows, a National Nature Reserve, with elevated walkways, where you can see a wide variety of unusual birds and wildlife. There are two castles in the bay – the mock-fortified, Tudor mansion known as Oxwich Castle, which is near the town and open to visitors, and the 12th-century Pennard Castle, situated on the cliff at the back of the beach where the Pennard Pill flows into the sea. There are lots of amenities on the foreshore, from parking to kiosks, and many good walks inland around the bay.

INFORMATION

Beach Type	Sand
Facilities	Toilets (with disabled facilities) and a shop
Activities	A variety of watersports available (Euphoria Sailing: 01792 234502). Oxwich Castle (01792 390359) is nearby
Parking	Pay parking available
Information	Swansea Tourist Information Centre (01792 468321) or the Penwith Estate (01792 390006)
Lifeguard Cover	July, August and certain busy weekends
Dogs	Welcome all year
Useful Websites	www.enjoygower.com www.mumbles.co.uk

INFORMATION

Beach Type	Sand
Facilities	Toilets (with disabled facilities), a café, shops and pub are situated at the top of the (steep) access path
Activities	Kite hire (Pitton Cross Camp Site: 01792 390593), surfboard hire (Bay Bistro: 01792 390519) and adventure tours (Gower Coast Adventure: 07866 250440)
Parking	Pay parking is available
Information	Swansea Tourist Information Centre (01792 468321) or the National Trust Office (01792 390707)
Lifeguard Cover	None
Dogs	Welcome all year
Useful Websites	www.visitswanseabay.com www.mumbles.co.uk

Rhossili Bay

NEAREST TOWN SWANSEA

Gower was the first area in Britain to be designated an Area of Outstanding Natural Beauty in 1956, and the south of the peninsula is justly prized for its stunning scenery of limestone cliffs, divided by sandy and rocky bays. The largest and most beautiful of these is Rhossili Bay, a beach of superlatives, its golden sands stretching for over 3 miles (5km), and with the highest peak in the Gower – the Beacon at 633ft (193m) – on Rhossili Down moors behind.

There's a steep path down to the long, crescent-shaped bay with breathtaking vistas across the Atlantic swells. It's a hard walk, which perhaps accounts for the fact that the beach is often quieter than you'd expect. At the southern end there's the mile-long tidal island of Worm's Head, which rises from the waters like a square-headed mythical beast – you can walk to it during two hours either side of low tide without getting your feet wet. The rocks on Worm's Head are full of nesting seabirds, and you might see a rare cushion starfish or even a grey seal – look out too for the natural, heart-shaped arch called Devil's Bridge.

As Gower's most westerly beach, Rhossili Bay is popular with surfers, especially at the northern end where the biggest rollers come in. There are various wrecks on the beach – you can see the skeletal wooden ribs of the *Helvetia*, destroyed in 1887, and the 1840 remains of the *City of Bristol* are visible at low tide near Burry Holms at the beach's northern tip.

There is a Bronze Age burial site on Rhossili Down, and the limestone cliffs around the coast from Worm's Head are dotted with deep, once-inhabited caves. In the Goat's Hole Cave at Paviland, a 29,000-year-old human skeleton called the 'Red Lady of Paviland' (later discovered to be a young male) was found in 1823.

Rhossili Bay is a place of history and such wild, awe-inspiring beauty that it's no wonder legends about it abound. The ghost of cruel Squire Mansell is said to drive his carriage and horses along the sands at night in search of

wrecked gold, and the spectre of Reverend John Ponsonby Lucas, who once lived in the lonely Rectory overlooking the beach, is often heard galloping to help his needy but long-dead parishioners.

In daylight though, Rhossili Bay is an unspoilt paradise, a day spent here is nicely rounded off with a cream tea at the Worm's Head Hotel, with its panoramic views of the bay and the paragliders launching 600ft (182m) off Rhossili Down.

Saundersfoot

NEAREST TOWN SAUNDERSFOOT

A few miles north of Tenby is the pretty seaside resort of Saundersfoot, set in a crescent-shaped bay, sweeping from Monkstone Point to rocky Wiseman's Bridge and Amroth beyond. There are several beaches along the bay, each with its own distinctive charm. Saundersfoot main beach sits in front of the apartments and cafés of The Strand, alongside the harbour, which is packed all-year round with fishing, sailing and power boats. The beach is wide and sandy with sheltered, shallow waters that offer good swimming and facilities for watersports. It's a very attractive spot for a family bucket-and-spade day out.

In its 19th-century industrial heyday, Saundersfoot harbour shipped anthracite coal from nearby mines in Stepaside: the coal was carried along the coast through tunnels in the cliff faces – today you can walk through these tunnels to access Saundersfoot's northerly beaches. Through the first tunnel you come to Coppet Hall beach (pictured), which is smaller and more secluded than the main beach, with rocky pools at low tides. It's a popular spot for windsurfing, kayaking and kite-surfing, as there is also access to the beach from a car park at the rear. You can continue through the railway tunnels to the unusual lava rock formations at Wiseman's Bridge, where there is a hotel and great views south-east over to Worm's Head and Rhossili Bay in the Gower Peninsula.

Beach Type	Sand
Facilities	Toilets (with disabled facilities), cafés, ice cream parlours, pubs, restaurants, shops, slipway, first aid post and several camp sites
Activities	No organised activities
Parking	Pay parking (including disabled access). Free roadside parking opposite the beach
Information	Saundersfoot Tourist Information Centre (01834 813672). This is situated in the main car park
Lifeguard Cover	May to September
Dogs	Banned between May and September on the main beach
Useful Websites	www.visit-saundersfoot.com www.visitpembrokeshire.com

Barafundle Bay

NEAREST TOWN STACKPOLE

On the south coast of craggy Pembrokeshire, tucked away beside Stackpole Head, is one of Britain's most beautiful beaches. Barafundle Bay regularly comes out top in good beach guides, and has been voted one of the 12 best beaches in the world. Perhaps it's the combination of remoteness (there is no car access) and the almost Mediterranean beauty of the turquoise waters, yellow sands and emerald, tree-lined shore that make this beach so special.

It takes an effort to get there: you have to walk up a steep path from the 18th-century Stackpole Quay to reach the Pembrokeshire coastal path – from where there are stunning views of Manorbier and Caldy Island to the east, and south to the lighthouse on Lundy Isle, on a clear day. Follow the path for about 15 minutes to get your first view of Barafundle Bay, then climb down the steep steps to arrive on its tranquil shores.

At any time, except in high summer, you'll probably have the beach to yourself. The sands shelve quickly making it a good swimming spot, and when the tide is out you can explore the gullies and caves around the cliff edges. Barafundle Bay is completely unspoilt: there are no ice cream vans, cafés, in fact no facilities at all – it feels as if you are in a secret world. The beach is managed by the National Trust as part of Stackpole Estate. For a longer walk, head south around Stackpole Head towards Broad Haven beach and the secluded Mere Pool valley. Then make your way back to the tiny harbour of Stackpole Quay for a well-deserved cream tea in the Boathouse tearoom.

Beach Type	Sand
Facilities	Toilets (with disabled facilities) and café are available in the car park by Stackpole Quay
Activities	No organised activities
Parking	Parking available (charges apply during the summer) in Stackpole Quay
Information	Pembroke Tourist Information Centre (01437 776499)
Lifeguard Cover	None
Dogs	Welcome all year
Useful Websites	www.visitpembrokeshire.com www.explorepembrokeshire.com www.pembrokeshirecoast.org.uk

Beach Type	Sand
Facilities	None on the beach, only in the local village
Activities	No organised activities
Parking	Pay parking available
Information	Haverfordwest Tourist Information Centre (01437 763110)
Lifeguard Cover	None
Dogs	Welcome all year
Useful Websites	www.marloessands.ukfossils.co.uk
	www.visitpembrokeshire.com
	www.welshwildlife.org

Marloes Sands

NEAREST TOWN MILFORD HAVEN

Marloes Sands, tucked away on one of Pembrokeshire's most westerly peninsulas, is a beautiful, isolated treasure. You have to walk for ten minutes or so down a cliff path to reach the beach, so it tends to be peaceful even in the height of summer. The spacious golden sands – perfect for sandcastle building and beach games – stretch out below the sloping cliffs, with dramatic, jagged rock formations occasionally emerging from the sand. At the north end of the beach, the rocks curve out to sea to create a backbone-shaped offshore island called Gateholm, which you can explore at low tide.

The beach is one of Britain's best for exploring rock pools: the rocks, dating from four distinct geological periods, are formed into striking vertical strata and arches, and you'll find lots of unusual sea beasts and colourful seaweeds. From the shore you can see nearby Skokholm and Skomer Islands, both nature reserves, with grey seals and huge colonies of nesting seabirds including the secretive manx shearwaters (Skomer has probably the largest colony in the world), puffins, gannets, razorbills, guillemots and storm petrels. Bird and nature lovers can take day trips to the islands (although you need to book well ahead for Skokholm, see www.welshwildlife.org) from the sheltered inlet of Martin's Haven just around the coast.

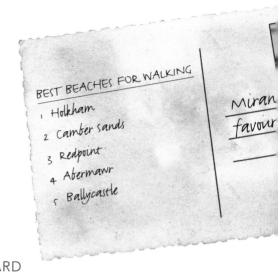

Abermawr

NEAREST TOWN FISHGUARD

This secluded, hard-to-reach beach is on the most westerly peninsula of Wales between Fishguard and St. David's Head – access is by a single-track road from Mathry, 2½ miles (4km) inland. The beach is in a small natural bay, with low, earth cliffs behind: it's stony at high tide but when the waters recede a deep stretch of dark sand is revealed. There's good swimming and interesting rockpools and a submerged prehistoric forest just offshore – preserved tree trunks can be seen in the water at low tide – scientists think it was created by floods of melting water around 6,000BC. Various Mesolithic flints and tools have been excavated, suggesting that the area was inhabited by mid-Stone Age hunter gatherers.

Behind the beach lies a swathe of green fields, marshlands and beautiful bluebell woods – take the circular 1½-mile (2.4km) walk through the woods from the beach. Abermawr is a wonderful place to come for solitude, scenery and adventure: there's a tough 12 mile (19km) walk down the Pembrokeshire coast path to Abereiddi, where you'll find the remarkable Blue Lagoon, a former deepwater quarry now used for canoeing and sub aqua diving.

Abermawr beach is good for sea angling, kiting and, when the swell is right, surfing (but be careful of the rip currents). Afterwards, head back up to the Farmers Arms in Mathry – it's a friendly, traditional country pub, and the best eating spot for miles around.

INFORMATION

Beach Type	Sand and pebble
Facilities	None, the nearest facilities can be found in Mathry
Activities	No organised activities
Parking	Limited roadside parking available
Information	Fishguard Tourist Information Centre (01437 776636)
Lifeguard Cover	None
Dogs	Welcome all year
Useful websites	www.visitpembrokeshire.com

Beach Type   Sand

Facilities   Toilets (with disabled facilities), café, shops, first aid post, camp site and caravan park (Cardigan Bay Holiday Park: 01239 615614). St. Dogmaels is the nearest village and has a variety of additional amenities on offer

Activities   No organised activities

Parking   Pay parking (with disabled access)

Information   Newport National Park Information Centre (01239 820912)

Lifeguard Cover   End of June to beginning of September

Dogs   Restrictions between 1st May and 30th September

Useful Websites   www.visitpembrokeshire.com

Poppit Sands

NEAREST TOWN CARDIGAN

The spectacular 186 mile (299km) long Pembrokeshire coastal path starts at Poppit Sands, the county's most northerly beach. It's a very popular beach with wide sands stretching out into the Teifi estuary. A few miles upstream is the historic town of Cardigan, where the first Eisteddfod was held in 1176 by Rhys ap Gruffydd, known as The Lord Rhys. The beach is backed by sand dunes and cliffs, with views over to tiny Cardigan Island, a nature reserve with a resident colony of grey seals – look out for the white baby seals in autumn. Guillemots, fulmars, shags and cormorants nest in the precipitous cliff faces, and you might see the occasional red kite. Around the estuary, bottlenose dolphins chase the salmon and sea trout that are heading to spawn in the River Teifi, a fisherman's paradise.

At low tide, the hard-packed sands stretch out for half a mile or more and are popular for kite buggying. However, there are strong and unpredictable tides and currents in the estuary, and care is needed when swimming – during the summer there is a lifeguard on the beach. There are also cafés, an RNLI lifeboat station and shop, and a good fish and chip shop in the nearby village of St. Dogmaels.

Beach Type	Sand
Facilities	Toilets (with disabled facilities and baby changing), showers, cafés, shops and a slipway
Activities	There are zoned areas for water sports and the Cardigan Bay Watersports Centre is located on the beach (01545 561257)
Parking	Pay parking (with disabled access)
Information	New Quay Tourist Information Centre (01545 560865)
Lifeguard Cover	July to August
Dogs	Restrictions between 1st May and 30th September
Useful Websites	www.newquay-westwales.co.uk www.tourism.ceredigion.gov.uk

New Quay Harbour

NEAREST TOWN NEW QUAY

There are three safe and sandy beaches and a harbour in the small fishing port of New Quay in Cardigan Bay. Harbour Beach has golden sands, safe swimming and a lifeguard patrol in summer. The picturesque, steeply terraced town tumbling down to the waterfront is most likely the inspiration for Llareggub (read it backwards) in Dylan Thomas's 'play for voices', Under Milk Wood: he lived in New Quay with his wife Caitlin during 1944-5. It's a lovely spot for family holidays, not least because this is one of the best places in Wales for sighting bottlenose dolphins (pictured left). There is a pod of 130 or so in the bay, and you can often see them from the shore, hunting or playing in the waves.

There are daily cruises along the beautiful Ceredigion Marine Heritage Coast to Birds Rock, The Caves and Seal's Bay, where you can see harbour porpoises, grey seals and numerous birds including red kites, razorbills and guillemots. Although most of the boats in the harbour are leisure craft, there is a local fishing industry catching lobsters, scallops and crabs, which you can buy at the fishmongers, or eat in the many restaurants and cafés. In Cardigan Bay Watersports Centre, near the harbour, you can learn to sea kayak, sail, powerboat, surf and windsurf. There are also excellent walks along the shore and cliffs on the Ceredigion coast path.

Aberaeron South

NEAREST TOWN ABERAERON

Aberaeron is one of the prettiest towns in Wales, an architectural gem full of colourwashed Georgian houses, wide streets and a stone-walled harbour, with fishing and pleasure boats bobbing around. Sailing is a popular and important part of life in Aberaeron. Beside the harbour is the beach of Aberaeron South, a spread of shingle with sand at low tide, with low-lying clay cliffs behind. You can sail, windsurf and canoe from the beach (bring your own equipment), and, on a clear day, you can see the cliffs of the Llyn peninsula in the distance. There's a car park beside a small slate-patterned weigh house – a reminder of the town's past prosperity as a port. The town has a craft centre and is famous for its honey ice cream that comes in exotic flavours (gooseberry, melon and ginger, passionfruit, soya and chocolate), and which has been made by the Holgate family for four decades.

The surrounding area is superb for walking; you can head north or south along the cliffs on the stunning Ceredigion coastal path, or there's a delightful inland walk through the woods along the banks of the River Aeron past Lovers' Bridge and an old mill ditch. Just 2½ miles (4km) further along is the National Trust house at Llanerchaeron, a villa designed by John Nash in the 1790s, with a self-sufficient estate including a dairy, brewery and salting house. Today it's an organic home farm where you can see lambing and haymaking.

INFORMATION

Beach Type	Shingle
Facilities	Toilets (with disabled facilities), a slipway and the town is just a few minutes away on foot for shops and cafés
Activities	No organised activities
Parking	Free roadside parking in Aberaeron town or pay parking also available close to the beach
Information	Aberaeron Tourist Information Centre (01545 570602)
Lifeguard Cover	None
Dogs	Restrictions apply between May and September. The South Beach has restrictions all year
Useful Websites	www.tourism.ceredigion.gov.uk

Harlech

NEAREST TOWN HARLECH

Harlech Castle stands on a rocky promontory overlooking the huge expanse of Harlech beach. The golden sands below are 4 miles (6.5km) long and provide a truly superb spot for walking, beachcombing, kite-surfing and bathing. The sands are backed by a dune system that has been accreting over the years – the castle was built next to the sea, but is now almost a mile from the shoreline because of longshore drift.

On the northern side of the beach and into the Dwyryd estuary, the mountainous dunes, mud flats and salt marshes of Morfa Harlech have been designated a National Nature Reserve, and a haven for rare plant species, birds and wildlife. At the southern end, near Llandbedr, lies the promontory of Shell Island (also known as Mochras), where more than 200 different kinds of shells have been found. Leatherback turtles are occasionally found in the seas, searching for jellyfish, which are abundant in the bay. Harlech Castle is well worth a visit, and a short drive around the estuary is Portmeirion, the fanciful Italianate village built by architect Clough Williams-Ellis between 1925 and 1975. The hotel there does remarkably good afternoon teas.

INFORMATION

Beach Type	Sand
Facilities	Toilets (with disabled access), shops, leisure centre and there are many camp sites in the area
Activities	No organised activities. Harlech Castle (01766 780552) is worth a visit
Parking	Pay parking available
Information	Harlech Tourist Information Centre (01766 780658)
Lifeguard Cover	None
Dogs	Restrictions apply 1st May to 30th September
Useful Websites	www.harlech.com www.walesdirectory.co.uk

INFORMATION

Beach Type	Sand
Facilities	Nearest facilities are in the nearby town
Activities	Abersoch Sailing School (01766 512981) offers a variety of activities
Parking	Pay parking available
Information	Abersoch Tourist Information Centre (01766 780658)
Lifeguard Cover	None
Dogs	Allowed only on the beach south of the slipway
Useful Websites	www.abersoch.co.uk

Abersoch

NEAREST TOWN ABERSOCH

The bustling town of Abersoch is tucked away on the south-east side of the Llyn peninsula, centrally placed in a superb bay, with long, sandy beaches and stunning views of St. Tudwal's islands just offshore. Abersoch is the sailing hub of the area: the Afon Soch flows into the sea at the harbour, which is the main launching spot for sailing and leisure boats. In summer you'll often see children crabbing off the harbour wall.

To the south, in front of the town, is Abersoch's main beach of golden sands, backed with low dunes and beach huts, some of which are available to rent. This beach has spectacular views over the bay to the mountains of West Wales, and is a water sports haven for sailing, windsurfing, wake-boarding, waterskiing and body-boarding. There are protected swimming areas away from the launching slips, cafés and toilets, and lots of good shops and facilities in town.

Paddle around the harbour to the north and you get to Quarry beach, which is quieter, with lovely safe swimming. You can take pleasure boat trips from Abersoch to St. Tudwal's and Bardsey Island – an early Celtic Christian island where 20,000 saints are supposed to be buried – at the southern tip of the peninsula. Look out for grey seals, bottlenose dolphins, puffins and on the sheer black cliffs, rare choughs (red-legged crows, pictured right).

Beach Type	Sand and pebbles
Facilities	None, nearest facilities in Llanengan village
Activities	A variety of watersports available (West Coast Surf: 01758 713067)
Parking	Free parking available approximately 300 metres away from the beach. Vehicular access to the beach is not permitted. No disabled spaces, but has a Tarmac surface
Information	Abersoch Tourist Information Centre (01758 712929)
Lifeguard Cover	None
Dogs	Welcome, but please be responsible
Useful Websites	www.gwynedd.com www.abersochtouristinfo.co.uk

Hell's Mouth

NEAREST TOWN ABERSOCH

The southern end of the Llyn Peninsula is spectacular, with black, craggy cliffs and long, sandy bays forming a 50 mile (80km) Heritage Coastline and Area of Outstanding Natural Beauty. Hell's Mouth (also known as Porth Neigwl) is the longest bay of all, almost 4 miles (6.5km) of golden, dune-backed sand facing huge Atlantic swells from the south-west. It's generally acknowledged to be the best surfing beach in North Wales, and in summer can be crowded with surfers and windsurfers taking advantage of the clear blue, shallow seas and powerful rollers and wedges. Although only 2½ miles (4km) from Abersoch, the beach is remote and is approached by a small road from Llanengan village (where you will find the15th-century church of St. Einion and the Sun Inn, which serves food), with parking on the earth cliffs about 320yd (300m) away.

When tides are big in spring and autumn, the sea angling is excellent – bass, flatfish, whiting, dabs, coalfish and rays are often caught – although the massive swells mean that debris and seaweed, unfortunately, gets dumped on the beach throughout the year. It's a lovely walk around the coastal path on the Cilan headland to the small, sandy cove of Porth Ceiriad nearby, a National Trust beach accessed by steep steps down the high cliffs, and another popular surfing destination.

Llanddwyn Bay

NEAREST TOWN MENAI BRIDGE

Beaches don't get much better than Llanddwyn Bay: the journey to the sand through the pine trees of Newborough forest (by toll road from the village of Newborough) is picturesque, there's an historic island just offshore, and the whole area forms a National Nature Reserve. Once you've parked in the large car park near the beach, walk through the dunes and take a right turn onto the long, golden stretch of sand. The beach shelves gently and is very safe for swimming. In the distance you'll see Llanddwyn island, which is steeped in history and legend. You can walk across the sands at low tides to see the ruins of a 15th-century church on the site of the oratory, built 1,000 years earlier by St. Dwynwen – she is the Welsh patron saint of lovers, said to have retired to the island with a broken heart. The sandy coves there are wonderfully secluded retreats, and from the cliff tops near the lighthouse and pilots' cottages at the far end you get stunning views over to Snowdonia and the Llyn Peninsula.

Walking back to the main sands of Llanddwyn Bay, stop and admire the crashing waves on the pine and dune-backed sands of Malltraeth beach to the left. It's a good spot to catch sight of unusual birds from nearby Malltraeth marshes, many of them painted by the famous naturalistic artist Charles Tunnicliffe, who lived nearby. His work is on display in the Oriel Gallery in Llangefni.

INFORMATION

Beach Type	Sand
Facilities	Toilets (with disabled facilities) available
Activities	No organised activities
Parking	Pay parking available
Information	Llanfairpwll Tourist Information Centre (01248 713177)
Lifeguard Cover	None
Dogs	Restrictions apply between March and September
Useful Websites	www.visitanglesey.co.uk

INFORMATION

Beach Type	Sand and a rocky coast
Facilities	Toilets (with disabled facilities and baby changing). Picnic tables are available during the summer along with a seasonal café. There is a slipway ramp onto the beach
Activities	No organised activities
Parking	Roadside free parking (with disabled access) available
Information	Llanfairpwll Tourist Information Centre (01248 713177)
Lifeguard Cover	None, however there is a beach warden from Easter to the end of September
Dogs	Banned all year
Useful Websites	www.visitanglesey.co.uk

Porth Dafarch

NEAREST TOWN HOLYHEAD

Off the west coast of the island of Anglesey lies Holy Island (both islands are accessible by road), and on its south-west coast lies Porth Dafarch, a secluded, quiet cove about 110yd (100m) wide. It is a sandy beach and has excellent facilities including a slipway onto the beach, picnic tables, toilets and good quality bathing water.

However, it's the site itself that captures the imagination: surrounded by cliffs, the rock formations have created interesting rock pools and rock faces – children love playing amongst the pools and shore divers often explore the underwater crevices and gullies. Experienced divers can also dive to the wreck of the *Missouri*, a three-masted ship sunk in 1886, which lies half a mile offshore. The beach is used by kayakers and dinghy sailors too.

In the field behind the beach there is an unmarked neolithic hut circle site, dating from the same period as the well-known Ty Mawr hut circles nearby. Walk north-west along the dramatic Anglesey coastal path and you reach Ty Mawr and South Stack, a tiny island with a lighthouse and precipitous cliffs on every side. There are about 400 steps down to the island or you can watch the 4,000 birds – including puffins, kittiwakes, guillemots and razorbills – nesting on the cliffs from the RSPB information centre at Ellins Tower (binoculars and telescopes are provided). The views are extraordinary.

Llandudno ✓

NEAREST TOWN LLANDUDNO

[handwritten: MARVELLOUS, TIMES HERE]

N estling into the west side of the limestone headland of Great Orme, and well away from the pier, donkey rides and old-fashioned delights of the North Shore, lies Llandudno's quieter, sand-duned West Shore. From this vast expanse of dark sand – when the tide goes out you can walk half a mile or more down to the sea – there are unrivalled views across to the island of Anglesey and down the Conway estuary, where Edward I built the beautiful, turreted Conway Castle in the 13th century. Llandudno West Shore is perhaps best known for its links with Alice Liddell, the girl who inspired Lewis Carroll's *Alice's Adventures in Wonderland*. She and her family used to holiday at Pen Morfa, a house just off the beach (now apartments), and there is a sculpture in her honour beside the model boating pond on the promenade.

You can walk or drive the 4 miles (6.5km) around Great Orme's Marine Drive from the North Shore to the West Shore, stopping en route for tea at the Old Rectory Tea Gardens on the road up to St. Tudno's church. Visit the Bronze Age Great Orme copper mines (you can access the underground tunnels that now house a museum) and walk up the summit of Great Orme: it's well worth the trip for the views alone. Alternatively, you can take the cable tramway up Great Orme from the ornamental gardens of Happy Valley.

[handwritten: ESTATIC]

Beach Type	Sand
Facilities	Toilets available by the beach. Llandudno is a short walk away providing a variety of additional amenities
Activities	No organised activities
Parking	Pay parking available
Information	Llandudno Tourist Information Centre (01492 876413)
Lifeguard Cover	None
Dogs	Restricted access from March to October
Useful Websites	www.visitllandudno.org.uk

Old Colwyn
NEAREST TOWN COLWYN BAY

This north-facing beach forms part of long, sandy Colwyn Bay, stretching from Rhos on Sea to the low protruding cliffs of Penmaen Rhos 3 miles (5km) away. The beach is golden sand, backed by a wide sweeping promenade, plenty of seating, refreshment kiosks and car parking. Old Colwyn is at the eastern end of the bay, with a steep-sided valley above. The bay gets very busy in summer, with jet skiing, sailing and other water sports. There's good sea fishing off the rocks at Penmaen Rhos.

Much of the town and surrounding land is within a conservation area. You can follow a nature and historical trail up the River Colwyn valley from the promenade through the Victorian-named Fairy Glen nature reserve and Tan-y-Coed gardens, which are overlooked by the ruins of a small castle tower. At the top of the cliffs, there are wonderful sea views: you can often see as far as the hills of south Scotland, and, on a clear night, the lights of Blackpool Tower sparkle in the distance. There is a cycle track running along the coast: follow it east to the Victorian pier and the tiny chapel of St. Trillo's at Rhos, founded in the 6th century – only about six people can squash into its congregation at any one time.

Beach Type	Sand
Facilities	Toilets (with disabled facilities), promenade and refreshment kiosks
Activities	Colwyn Jet Ski Club (01745 852093) and Pleasure Cruises (07961 561589) operate in the area
Parking	Free parking (with disabled access)
Information	Llandudno Tourist Information Centre (01492 876413)
Lifeguard Cover	None
Dogs	Restrictions between May and September
Useful Websites	www.old-colwyn-beach.wales.info

northern ireland

Only three of Northern Ireland's six counties –
Londonderry, Antrim and Down – border its
breathtakingly diverse coastline, which stretches
from the rugged cliffs and golden sands of
Londonderry's Downhill in the west to the gentler,
dune-backed beach of County Down's Tyrella,
near the purple-hazed Mountains of Mourne.
On the north coast of County Antrim is the
UNESCO World Heritage Site of the Giant's
Causeway, a stretch of basalt columns formed
by rapidly cooling lava 60 million years ago, and
today the most visited site in Ireland, attracting
half a million people a year. So extraordinary are
these 40,000 weathered shapes – with names such
as the Pipe Organ and Giant's Boot – that legend
has it they were formed by the Irish giant Finn
MacCool and his Scottish rival Benandoner battling
it out across the Sea of Moyle.

Along the cliffs and headlands from Portstewart
to Ballycastle runs the 33 mile (53km) Causeway
Coast Way, punctuated by ruined castles and forts
at Dunluce, Dunseverick and Kenbane; limestone
caves and arches at White Rocks; a long and
wobbly rope bridge to Carrick-a-Rede Island;

Portstewart •

Downhill •

NORTHERN IRELAND

and spectacular views to offshore Rathin Island and the Scottish coast. The scenery in County Down on the east coast is gentler, with fishing villages, sandy beaches at Tyrella and Dundrum Bay, and the 6,000-year-old dunes at Murlough National Nature Reserve, where you can see unusual plants and wildlife. Finally, you reach Slieve Donard, Northern Ireland's highest peak, in the dramatic Mountains of Mourne just a few miles from the sea. It's a long walk up, but from the top you get breathtaking views of this extraordinary coastline.

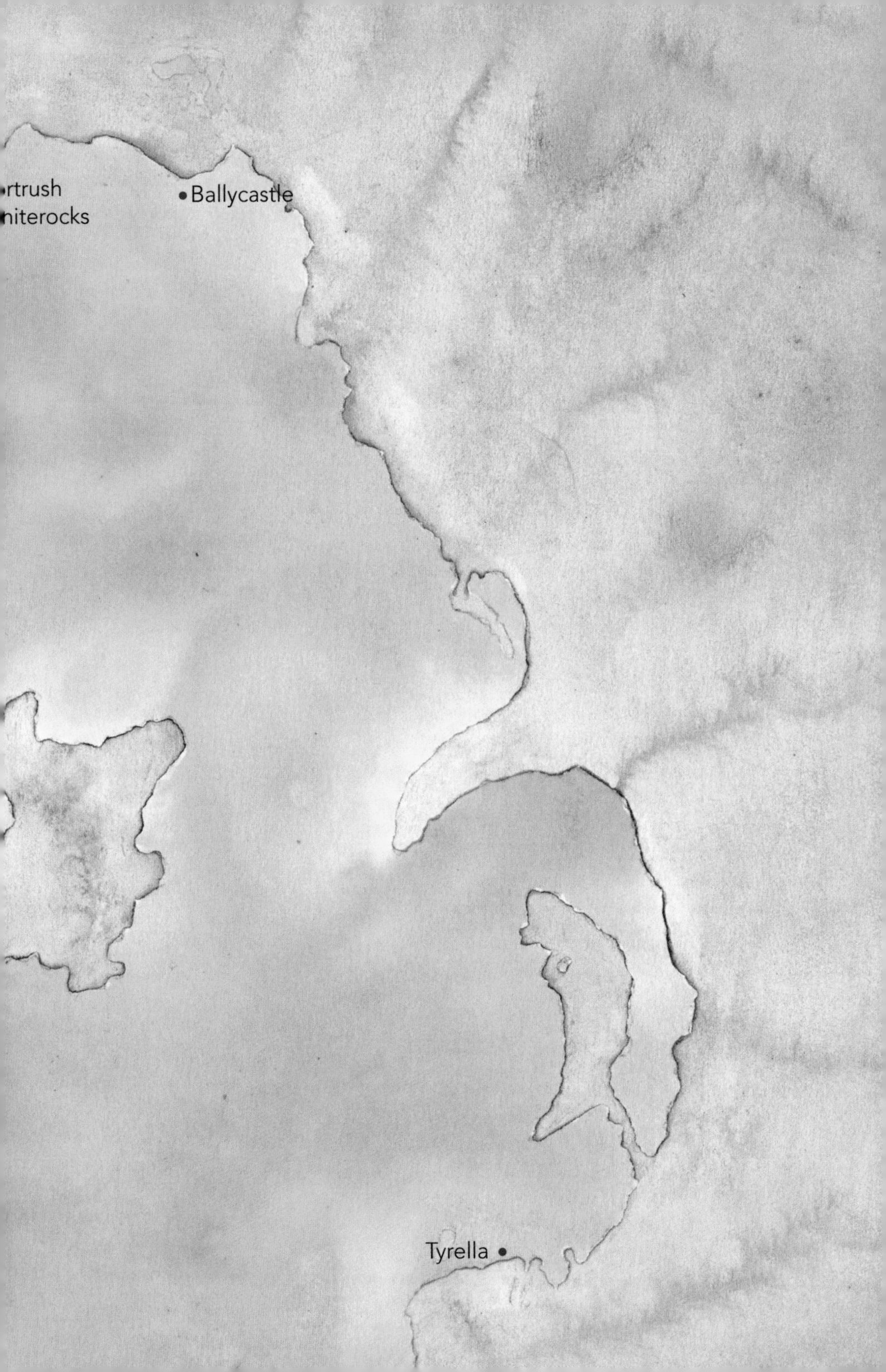

rtrush
niterocks

Ballycastle

Tyrella

INFORMATION

Beach Type	Sand
Facilities	Toilets (with disabled facilities), first aid station and lost child centre, shops, seasonal catering by mobile vans
Activities	No organised activities, watersports zoning in place
Parking	Pay parking available
Information	Downpatrick Tourist Information Centre (028 4461 2233) or Delamont Country Park (028 4482 8333)
Lifeguard Cover	Weekends from Easter and daily in July and August
Dogs	Not permitted from 1st May to 30th September
Useful Websites	www.discovernorthernireland.com www.irishsecrets.ie/visitor-secrets

Tyrella
NEAREST TOWN DOWNPATRICK

The lovely Dundrum Bay is probably the best seaside area of the south-eastern coast of Northern Ireland, and Tyrella, with its 1½ miles (2.5km) of golden sands, is easily the best beach. A large and ancient area of dunes, thought to have originated over 8,000 years ago, and now designated a conservation area, renowned for sea holly and pyramidal orchids, backs the flat sands. The nearest village of Minerstown, just to the east of Tyrella, with its caravan parks and shops, is the busiest part of the bay. Take some binoculars with you if you're walking along the beach as you might catch sight of grey and common seals (pictured right) in the waters. Head further east towards St. John's Point and lighthouse and then look back for excellent views of the blue-grey Mountains of Mourne to the south west. The beach is perfect for family fun in the sun and long lovely walks whatever the weather (although keep to the well-marked paths in the dunes). There are toilet facilities and a beach centre; the sand is very well maintained by the local council, helping Tyrella to win many awards. It's also a popular surfing and kite-surfing beach.

Ballycastle

NEAREST TOWN BALLYCASTLE

The coast of north Antrim is spectacular, boasting the Giant's Causeway, the gateway to the Glens of Antrim and Ballycastle beach, with views on a clear day over to the Mull of Kintyre. The beach is set in a bay framed to the east by the sheer 600ft (183m) cliffs of Fair Head headland (the most north-easterly point of Ireland), while to the west, the ruins of Kinbane Castle sit on an imposing limestone outcrop. The sand is slightly coarse and gravelly, which makes it perfect for walking if you don't want to sit or swim. There's a promenade and seafront at Ballycastle with tennis courts, and an inner harbour and marina. In the distance offshore sits the small inhabited island of Rathlin – take one of the daily boat trips to go bird-watching or diving, to see one of the many wrecks that lie beneath the treacherous waters around the island. Every August the small town of Ballycastle hosts the Ould Lammas Fair, the largest horse fair in Ireland which began in the 17th century, and is also famous for dulse, an edible seaweed, and Yellowman toffee.

Beach Type	Sand
Facilities	Toilets (with disabled facilities), first aid, promenade, harbour and leisure centre
Activities	Tennis courts are available for hire (028 2076 3300) and the Annual Tennis Competition is held in August. Boat trips run from the harbour
Parking	Free parking available
Information	Ballycastle Tourist Information Centre (028 2076 2024)
Lifeguard Cover	None
Dogs	Restricted access between May and September
Useful Websites	www.moyle-council.org

INFORMATION

Beach Type	Sand
Facilities	Toilets (with disabled facilities)
Activities	Organised watersports are available at the Portrush end of the beach (Troggs Watersports: 028 7082 5476). A variety of boat trips leave from Portrush Harbour during the summer
Parking	Free parking available
Information	Portrush Tourist Information Centre (028 7082 3333)
Lifeguard Cover	July, August and the first two weekends in September
Dogs	Restrictions apply, see local signage
Useful Websites	www.discovernorthernireland.com

Portrush Whiterocks

NEAREST TOWN PORTRUSH

This spectacular beach takes its name from the limestone cliffs that face the bay, which runs from Curran Strand to Dunluce Castle. The area is renowned for the fantastic caves and arches that dot the coast, with magical-sounding names like Shelagh's Head, Teardrop, the Lion's Paw and Elephant Rock. Some of the caves are interconnected, others stretch inland and run under the main road along the Portrush cliffs (the A2). The limestone rocks and white sands give the sea a crystal turquoise clarity, and surfers head out to breakers from the foot of the cliffs (note that there are a couple of rip tides that should be avoided if swimming). A coastguard station off the point of Ramore Head juts out from the town of Portrush like a finger, almost pointing at the rocky Skerries islets just off the coast. There are daily boat trips in and out of the caves, which are only accessible by sea, and if you're lucky you'll spot one of the many shipwrecks that shimmer beneath the clear waters of the bay. For history, trek to the romantic ruins of Dunluce Castle, to which you cross by a bridge over precipitous drops, and marvel at the men who built the 13th-century wonder.

BEST SPOTS FOR ROCK POOLS

1 Botany Bay

2 Portrush

3 Marloes Sands

4 Aberdour Silver Sands

5 Rhossili Bay (Worm's Head)

Miranda's favourites...

Portstewart

NEAREST TOWN PORTSTEWART

Portstewart is a more sedate, although slightly larger, town than neighbouring Portrush. Built for the most part in the 19th century, it became a favourite resort for the growing middle classes who flocked to the crescent-shaped seafront promenade, which sits between two rocky headlands and under the shadow of O'Hara's Castle (now a Catholic grammar school). The strand is a lovely 2 mile (3km) long stretch of white sand just to the west of the town, backed by the area's largest sand dunes and designated an Area of Special Scientific Interest – the marram grass is a haven for insects and wild flowers. The strand has been run by the National Trust since 1980, which operates car parking on the beach, zoned water sports areas and a new 'green' visitor centre with fabulous views of the coast. Venturing onto the strand, there is a well-marked, 3½ mile (5.5km) circular walk that takes you through the dunes, around the Bann estuary and along the river, with its wealth of birdlife, before heading back to the flat sands of the beach. Near the promenade there are children's play areas with swings and paddling pools, climbing frames – and lots of tasty seaside food on sale.

INFORMATION

Beach Type	Sand
Facilities	Toilets (with disabled facilities), shops, first aid point and information centre
Activities	This is a popular beach for watersports, bring your own equipment
Parking	Pay parking available
Information	Portrush Tourist Information Centre (028 7082 3333) or the National Trust office (028 2073 1582)
Lifeguard Cover	July and August
Dogs	Dogs on lead welcome
Useful Websites	www.discovernorthernireland.com

Downhill

NEAREST TOWN COLERAINE

This scenic stretch of golden sand is so named because it can only be reached downhill, of course. It forms part of Northern Ireland's most spectacular beach, stretching from Castlerock to Magilligan Point in the west, with miles of sand and turquoise sea backed by dramatic cliffs and waterfalls. Perched on the clifftop overlooking Downhill beach is Mussenden Temple, an 18th-century circular folly built by the flamboyant earl bishop, Frederick Hervey, and inspired by the Temple of Vesta at Tivoli. From the cliffs, the views are amazing: you can see three counties (Antrim, Londonderry and Donegal) and a fair way out to sea. The beach is popular with families, walkers, horse riders and surfers, with lovely clear waters and clean sand. You can explore the ruins of Hervey's country house (now run by the National Trust) above the beach, or walk in the estate where there are many rare trees, planted around a large, natural lake. For a day trip, take the ferry from Magilligan across Lough Foyle to Greencastle on the Inishowen peninsula in Eire (it takes 10 minutes, and saves a road trip of 48 miles/78km), which has rugged scenery and great pebble and shell beaches at Malin Head.

INFORMATION

Beach Type	Sand
Facilities	Toilets (with disabled facilities)
Activities	No organised activities, this is a popular beach for horseriding
Parking	Free parking
Information	Coleraine Tourist Information Centre (028 70347034)
Lifeguard Cover	July and August
Dogs	Restrictions apply, see local signage
Useful Websites	www.discovernorthernireland.com

scotland

(handwritten: YES! EVERY TIME!)

Scotland and its islands have an astonishing
11,550 miles (18,587km) of crenellated coastline,
an abundance of glorious sandy beaches, rocky
coves, cliffs, bays, islands and sea lochs. Some
of the most beautiful wilderness beaches in the
world are found here, their dazzling white sands
and aquamarine waters set against a backdrop
of sheer cliffs, purple-heathered mountains or vivid
green machair – a rare type of sand-dune pasture.

The mostly rocky eastern coast has several long
and attractive strands of sand including St.
Andrews West Sands, Lunan Bay and Brora. But
arguably, the most enticing Scottish beaches are
on the west coast, the Islands and in the Highlands.
Here the fine-grained sands, composed mainly
of shell fragments, are of a spectacular whiteness
and the beaches tend to be small and enclosed
by rugged headlands and vertiginous cliffs, like
the one at Calgary Bay on the Isle of Mull. There's
the occasional long beach such as Luskentyre on
Harris, but even on larger beaches you're often
alone, at one with nature – a third of Scottish
beaches have fewer than five visitors a day in
summer. However, if you're really looking for

Sandwood Bay • • S

Luskentyre •

Firemore • •

• Redpoint

• Applecross

Calgary Bay •

solitude, head for Sandwood or Sango Bay
on the north coast of Sutherland, a place
so close to wild Cape Wrath and the
northern expanse of the Atlantic,
you can feel as if you are falling
off the end of the earth.

The warming effect of the Gulf Stream
makes the west coast seas less perishingly cold
than you'd expect this far north, and even on the
east coast, you see hardy surfers and windsurfers
out catching the high rollers and big swells.
The wildlife around Scotland's coast is
uncommonly good, with golden eagles,
puffins, Atlantic salmon, bottlenose
dolphins, basking sharks, seals
and porpoises. And of course, there are the
famous golf courses adjoining the beaches,
including St. Andrews and Machrihanish – two
of the trickiest seaside golf courses in the world.

• Machrihanish Bay

Beach Type	Sand
Facilities	Toilets
Activities	Angling, surfing and other watersports popular here (Coast to Coast Surf School: 01368 869734). John Muir Country Park (01620 827421) and East Links Family Park (01368 863607)
Parking	Free parking available
Information	Visit Scotland (0845 2255121)
Lifeguard Cover	None
Dogs	Welcome, but must be kept on leads
Useful Websites	www.guide.visitscotland.com
	www.belhavenbay.org
	http://perfectday.visitscotland.com

Belhaven Bay
NEAREST TOWN DUNBAR

Belhaven Bay sits on a spectacular stretch of coast running from Dunbar 20 miles (32km) eastward, where storm-sculpted sandstone cliffs, alive with nesting birds, are interspersed with sandy beaches. Belhaven is one of these beaches, its wide sands backed by a high dune ridge, the perfect spot for making sandcastles, playing beach games and having a family day out. Surfers and kite fliers make the most of the crashing waves and high winds, and swimming is safe in calm weather (although jellyfish are often found here). This is, apparently, the sunniest and driest part of the Scottish coast. Edinburgh is only a 40-minute drive away, so expect day-trippers in the summer months, however the beach rarely gets overcrowded. Dunbar itself is full of history, from its cobbled Cromwell Harbour to the ruined castle and 17th-century Town House. There are also family-oriented activity centres nearby such as the East Links Family Park. The beach is part of the John Muir Country Park, which offers great walks, bird-watching and spectacular views out to Bass Rock.

Beach Type	Sand and shingle
Facilities	None, the nearest facilities are in Longniddry
Activities	No organised activities
Parking	Free parking available
Information	Visit Scotland (0845 2255121)
Lifeguard Cover	None
Dogs	Welcome all year, but be responsible
Useful Websites	www.eastlothian.gov.uk http://perfectday.visitscotland.com

Gosford Sands

NEAREST TOWN LONGNIDDRY

In the late 1960s the beach and dunes of Gosford Sands were being eroded by the elements, and a policy of thatching the sand with buckthorn and sea-lyme grass was introduced, which halted the decline. Today the bay, which sits between Longniddry to the west (the closest railway station) and Aberlady to the east, is part of one of the most popular visitor spots on the East Lothian coast as it is just a few miles away from Edinburgh. Its beautiful sands spread down to muddy expanses when the tide recedes, which make it a good habitat for wading birds such as grey plover (pictured left) and curlew. It's a great beach for kite flying and coastal walking – you can take the John Muir Way from Cockenzie to Aberlady passing Gosford Sands en route. South of the beach and in clear view sits the 18th-century Gosford Estate, its mansion built by Robert Adam for the 7th Earl of Wemyss whose family still live there. The house, which has an extensive art collection, is open to the public during the summer months.

INFORMATION	**Beach Type**	Sand
	Facilities	Toilets (with disabled and baby changing facilities), first aid station, café/restaurant, slip way
	Activities	This is a popular watersports spot. There is zoning for water sports and a picnic area
	Parking	Pay parking (with disabled access)
	Information	Visit Scotland (0845 2255121)
	Lifeguard Cover	July to August
	Dogs	Restrictions apply May to September
	Useful Websites	www.keepscotlandbeautiful.org
		http://perfectday.visitscotland.com

Aberdour Silver Sands

NEAREST TOWN ABERDOUR

There are two beaches in the picturesque village and resort of Aberdour on the northern side of the Firth of Forth. Silver Sands, with its fine bay backed by trees, then there's rockier Black Sands beach, which is on the other side of town. The fine, silver sands make the former a great family destination, with a bouncy castle and play area for children in summer, as well the best swimming in the region. There are usually seals dotting the rocks at sea, while in the pools along the shore you'll find butterfish, sea anemones, hermit crabs, periwinkles and whelks. Rocks are covered with beards of mussels, and the sky above is filled with terns, oystercatchers and other more common seabirds. A little way down the beach is Hawkcraig Point from where you can enjoy good views of the Firth of Forth railway bridge, and lots of rare wildflowers, too.

Between the two beaches, Aberdour's quaint harbour is full of sailing boats, and you can make trips out to the nearby islands, including Inchcolm, with the spectacular St. Colm's Abbey high on its tip, and Inchmickery for the birdlife. The town itself is set back behind the trees, with a 14th-century castle and the 12th-century church of St. Fillan's. Aberdour is situated on the Fife coastal path, and there's a self-contained 3 ¾ mile (6km) circular walk through the town and surrounding area.

INFORMATION

Beach Type	Sand
Facilities	Toilets (with disabled facilities), first aid post, shops and restaurants are close by
Activities	A variety of watersports available (East Neuk Outdoors: 01333 311929 or Elie Watersports: 01333 330962)
Parking	Pay parking (with disabled access)
Information	St. Andrews Tourist Information Centre (01334 472021) or Visit Scotland (0845 2255121)
Lifeguard Cover	July to August
Dogs	Restrictions from June to September
Useful Websites	www.keepscotlandbeautiful.org http://perfectday.visitscotland.com

St. Andrews West Sands

NEAREST TOWN ST. ANDREWS / NICE

When the tide is out and the sun is setting, nothing can beat the majestic view from West Sands over to the towers and spires of St. Andrews, with its ruined castle and cathedral standing above craggy, low-slung cliffs. The beach, a flat and beautiful stretch of uninterrupted sand on the northern coast of Fife, is famously the setting for the opening scene of the Oscar-winning film *Chariots of Fire*. The West Sands begin near the town, just past the Royal and Ancient golf clubhouse, and end at the estuary of the River Eden, a haven for birdlife two miles away. The beach is backed by dunes, behind which lie the town's links golf courses including the world-renowned Old Course, where the Open Championship is often held. The game of golf originated in St. Andrews and has been played on these seaside links for more than 450 years (there's an interesting history of golf museum nearby). Expect crowds of families on the beach in summer at the town end – the sand shelves making this a good beach for swimming – and lots of kite-boarders and sand yachters at the estuary end. St. Andrews University, founded in 1413, is Scotland's most ancient seat of learning and the third oldest university in Britain after Oxford and Cambridge, and the town's grey stone streets, harbour, pier and ruined cathedral are well worth a visit.

Beach Type	Sand
Facilities	None
Activities	No organised activities
Parking	Free parking available
Information	Montrose Tourist Information Centre (01674 673232) or Visit Scotland (0845 2255121)
Lifeguard Cover	None
Dogs	Welcome all year
Useful Websites	www.undiscoveredscotland.co.uk http://perfectday.visitscotland.com

Lunan Bay

NEAREST TOWN MONTROSE

At Lunan Bay there's a curving path from the car park to the top of the dunes; walk up and you'll hear the pounding of the waves before you see the 2½ miles (4 km) of glorious sand stretching out before you – this isn't called the 'singing sands' for nothing. To the north is the rocky headland of Boddin Point, to the south the low cliffs of Lang Craig, from where you get spectacular views of the coastline and the reefs around Inchcape Rock – the subject of Robert Southey's famous 1820 poem – and lighthouse, which was built in 1811 by Robert Stevenson, grandfather of author Robert Louis Stevenson. The beach itself is divided by the river mouth of the Lunan Water, and is overlooked by the dramatic ruins of Red Castle, built as a hunting lodge in the 12th century and devastated by attackers 400 years later. Today the beach is a popular spot for walkers, surfers, horse riders and bird-watchers – look out for great grey shrikes, red-backed shrikes (pictured right), scoters and even occasional hoopoes. The swimming is safe away from the river mouth and rocks, and at low tide you might find some pieces of agate and jasper, for which the beach is renowned, among the pebbles on the sand.

Montrose

NEAREST TOWN MONTROSE

The historic town of Montrose, set at the mouth of the South Esk River, is surrounded on three sides by sea water – the beach, the harbour and Montrose Basin, a natural tidal lagoon that has been a bird sanctuary since 1981. On the beach, golden sands stretch for 3 miles (5km) from Montrose to the North Esk River, with stunning views south to Scurdieness lighthouse. Montrose is a family beach with a promenade, car parking and cafés at the town end, and the Seafront Splash play area for children (1¼ mile/2km from town centre) with white sands, pools, trampolines, pitch and putt course and an ice-cream parlour. Walk north a little way and behind the dunes lies Montrose's Medal Golf Course, the fifth oldest golf course in the world, its links fringed with yellow-flowering gorse bushes. Montrose's elegant, broad streets are worth a tour – this is where the Old Pretender, James Stuart, spent his last night in Scotland after the failed uprising of 1715, and you can see the 'chevalier glass' he drank from in the museum.

A visit to Montrose Basin is a must. This 3 square mile (750ha) wildlife sanctuary attracts 50,000 migratory birds each year including pink-footed geese, wild whooper swans, osprey (pictured right), avocets and lesser yellowlegs. You can watch them all from the high-powered telescopes in the visitor centre (open April to October), and perhaps also catch sight of seals, otters, eels and salmon.

Beach Type	Sand
Facilities	Toilets (with disabled facilities), shops, cafés, restaurants, first aid, picnic tables, promenade and a camp site (South Links: 01674 672105)
Activities	Seafront splash play area for children, pitch and putt, and windsurfing is popular on this beach
Parking	Free parking (with disabled access)
Information	Montrose Tourist Information Centre (01674 673232) Visit Scotland (0845 2255121)
Lifeguard Cover	None
Dogs	Restrictions from May to September
Useful Websites	www.montrose.org.uk http://perfectday.visitscotland.com

Brora

The small, industrial village of Brora was established in the 16th century when locally mined coal was used in the extraction of salt from sea water. Today only a few boats sail from Brora's small harbour, but the promise of watching dolphins, minke whales, grey and common seals off the coast is what brings many people to this wild, beautiful place. The 2 mile (3km) beach is mostly golden sand with a shingle channel around the mouth of the Brora river, which flows into the North Sea here. Swimming is safe, except around the river mouth where there are Jurassic rocks deposited from upstream – these contain many fossils and you might find small ones on the beach after high seas or storms. There is a golf course overlooking the beach, designed in 1923 by Scotsman James Braid, and the town and car parks are close by. Brora beach is a highly rated family destination in any season; made only more enticing by the excellent Italian ice cream you can buy in Capaldi's.

Beach Type	Sand
Facilities	There is a picnic site; the village of Brora is close by for further facilites
Activities	No organised activities
Parking	Free parking
Information	Brora Heritage Centre (01408 622024) Visit Scotland (0845 2255121)
Lifeguard Cover	None
Dogs	Welcome all year
Useful Websites	http://perfectday.visitscotland.com

Beach Type	Sand and rock
Facilities	Toilets and a camp site nearby
Activities	A variety of surfing activities available (Thurso Surf: www.thursosurf.com)
Parking	Pay parking available
Information	Harbour Office (01847 892500) or Visit Scotland (0845 2255121)
Lifeguard Cover	None
Dogs	Welcome, but please be responsible
Useful Websites	www.thurso.ukfossils.co.uk http://perfectday.visitscotland.com

BEST BEACHES FOR WATERSPORTS

1 Abersoch
2 Hell's Mouth
3 Sennen Cove
4 Thurso
5 Hayling Island

Miranda's
favourites...

Thurso

NEAREST TOWN THURSO

Thurso is one of the most northerly towns in Britain, very close to John o' Groats and with views of the distant cliffs of Dunnet Head and the Orkney island of Hoy on a clear day. The town has had trading links with Scandinavia since the early Middle Ages; indeed its very name is thought to derive from Thor, the Norse god of thunder. Thurso is on a tidal estuary: the small, sandy beach on the eastern side of the river sits beneath the old town and the ruins of Thurso castle. The beach is remarkable for two reasons. Just a short walk eastwards towards Castletown you reach rocky plateaux and sandstone cliffs from the Devonian period, about 400 million years old. These rocks are full of fossilized blue and black fish, and although it's rare to come across a whole fish, you'll easily find scales, teeth and other fragments.

In winter and spring, Thurso turns into a world-class surfing beach. The huge swells of the Pentland Firth, the stretch of water between the mainland and the Orkney Islands (where orca and minke whales, seals, dolphins and porpoises can be seen) builds fast-barrelling waves, and various international surfing championships have been held here. Some say the waves are as good (if not as warm) as in Hawaii and other top surfing spots. If you visit in summer, Thurso also has some of the longest days in Britain – in midsummer the sun rises at 3am and sets 20 hours later.

Strathy Bay

NEAREST TOWN MELVICH

It's a wild, windy place that can be downright inhospitable in bad weather, but get there in spring or summer and it's beautiful. The wide, flat sands and rocks of the bay are backed by dunes and grassy slopes that are alive with wild flowers such as Scottish primrose, spring squill and kidney vetch. You can walk to Strathy Point on a road perched atop steep cliffs, and from there you can see as far as Orkney on a clear day, or as near as leaping dolphins and spouting whales, whatever the weather. The village of Strathy consists of a few scattered crofts, four churches (some of which are now holiday homes), a village hall and an inn, and there's a lighthouse on the point. Walking along the beach you will see caves and rock stacks formed by the wave power of a frequently unruly sea. Strathy Bay is remote and rugged and quite lovely, regardless of the weather.

Beach Type	Sand
Facilities	Toilets (with disabled facilities)
Activities	The Pentland Canoe Club (01847 831508) offers white water kayaking, sea touring, surfing and kayak surfing
Parking	Free parking available
Information	Visit Scotland (0845 2255121)
Lifeguard Cover	None
Dogs	Welcome, but please be responsible
Useful Websites	www.undiscoveredscotland.co.uk http://perfectday.visitscotland.com

Sango Bay

NEAREST TOWN DURNESS

Not far from Cape Wrath, Scotland's northernmost point, is secluded and sheltered Sango Bay. This remote spot is accessed only by a single-track road to the nearby village of Durness, the most north-westerly settlement in Britain (it takes about three and a half hours to drive here from Inverness). The sandy beach has rocky outcrops, but it's a safe swimming spot and there are often surfers enjoying the fun in the bay's clear waters. A little further east is Smoo Cave, located at the entrance to a steeply walled inlet. The intrepid might fancy a trip deep into the first chamber which is 66yd (60m) long and 44yd (40m) high; there's a waterfall – the chimney Smoo – in the second chamber, which you can view from a platform, but the third chamber is accessible only by boat. On the cliffs above the bay there's a caravan and camping site, with a restaurant, open from March to October – John Lennon apparently spent his summer holidays as a child in a croft nearby. You'll invariably find a geologist or two examining the rocks at Sango Bay, which are a part of an unusual formation called the Moine Thrust Belt, and the views from the cliffs are spectacular.

INFORMATION

Beach Type	Sand and rock
Facilities	The village is close by and offers excellent facilities
Activities	No organised activities, this is a popular surf spot
Parking	Free parking
Information	Durness Tourist Information Centre (01971 511259) Visit Scotland (0845 2255121)
Lifeguard Cover	None
Dogs	Welcome, but please be responsible
Useful Websites	www.undiscoveredscotland.co.uk http://perfectday.visitscotland.com

Beach Type	Sand
Facilities	None
Activities	No organised activities (you'll be tired from the walk!)
Parking	None
Information	Durness Tourist Information Centre (01971 511259) or Visit Scotland (0845 2255121)
Lifeguard Cover	None
Dogs	Welcome all year
Useful Websites	www.undiscoveredscotland.co.uk http://perfectday.visitscotland.com

Sandwood Bay

NEAREST TOWN TONGUE

S andwood Bay on the coast of Sutherland is about 10 miles (16km) from the most northerly point of Cape Wrath and is one of Scotland's remotest beaches. You have to walk 4 miles (6.5km) from Blairmore along a rough inland track with no sign of sea or sand until you reach the top of a steep ridge – then the mile-long, dune-backed bay stretches before you, flanked by high cliffs at each end. The effort is worth it. Huge Atlantic rollers crash onto the shore, making this a popular surfing spot (although the undertow means that it's dangerous to swim). Along the pinky-hued sands to the left you can see Am Buachaille, a towering sea stack 200ft (61m) high, which looks like a ship in full rig coming in to shore. Inland, behind the dunes and machair, there are the sparkling waters of freshwater Sandwood Loch. It's a stunning coastal wilderness and legends about it abound – look out for the beautiful mermaid sitting on the rocks and the old seafarer, wrecked centuries ago, who's said to prowl the ruins of Sandwood cottage near the beach in stormy weather.

Firemore
NEAREST TOWN POOLEWE

The aptly named Firemore Beach offers possibly the warmest swimming on Scotland's west coast. Near the River Ewe (famous for salmon fishing) and warmed by the Gulf Stream, the wide, reddish sandy beach is on the shore of Loch Ewe, a sea loch. Opposite the beach is the tiny Isle of Ewe. Firemore and Loch Ewe are great places for swimmers, sailors and families who love the outdoor life. You will find a camp site by the beach on a grassy bank (it has no facilities, but it costs very little to stay there). At the northern end of the loch, there's a lovely walk along the coastline of small hamlets, inlets and a harbour to a small settlement called Cove. There's hill walking for every level of rambler, lots of wildlife to spot, including long-haired Highland cattle, and golden eagles, buzzards and possibly rare sea eagles. Glass-bottomed boat trips are available around the loch and there's excellent fishing to be had, plus an indoor swimming pool at Poolewe if the water is too cold. You could also visit the sub-tropical gardens at Inverewe (run by the National Trust for Scotland), which are full of exotic plants including bamboo, eucalyptus and Himalayan rhododendrons.

Beach Type	Sand and rock
Facilities	Toilets and café
Activities	No organised activities
Parking	Free parking
Information	Visit Scotland (0845 2255121)
Lifeguard Cover	None
Dogs	Welcome, but please be responsible
Useful Websites	http://perfectday.visitscotland.com

Redpoint

NEAREST TOWN GAIRLOCH

To get to Redpoint, drive to Loch Gairloch and then take the single-track coast road south to Badachro and Opinan, passing wooded coves and bays with rocky foreshores, following the road around a rocky headland, where the rocks give way to a bay of bright red sand, backed by sea-eroded, odd-shaped dunes. On a clear day you can see the Isle of Skye from here. Three miles (5km) further south, you will find wide beaches facing Loch Torridon, another sea loch. If you want a quiet holiday, this is the place to go. Rarely will you see crowds of people here even during the height of summer, which is a surprise given the natural beauty of the area, the safe swimming beaches and remarkable skyline of multi-peaked mountain pinnacles of Beinn Alligin and Liathach across the loch. It's a truly stunning place, with over 16,000 acres (6,500ha) of land looked after by the National Trust for Scotland, and a wealth of birds and wildlife to be seen. There are walks to suit all levels, but the relatively gentle 7 mile (11km) route from Redpoint to Diabaig is a delight.

Beach Type	Sand and shingle
Facilities	None
Activities	No organised activities
Parking	Free parking available
Information	Gairloch Tourist Information Centre (01445 712130) or Visit Scotland (0845 2255121)
Lifeguard Cover	None
Dogs	Welcome all year, but be responsible
Useful Websites	www.undiscoveredscotland.co.uk http://perfectday.visitscotland.com

Luskentyre

NEAREST TOWN TARBERT

Sandy beaches don't come any better than Luskentyre, on the west coast of Harris in the Outer Hebrides. This wild, remote beach stretches for 3¼ miles (5.2km) from the enormous sand dunes of Luskentyre Banks – reaching up to 115ft (35m) high – to the long sand spit of Corran Seilebost in the south. At high tide the estuary is almost covered with water, but as it recedes a huge expanse of rippled, powdery white sand spreads out as far as the eye can see. Stand on the rocky southern end of Corran Seilebost and spread before you is one of Scotland's most magnificent vistas: dazzling sandflats and saltings backed by dunes and fertile grassy machair, the sea an impossibly brilliant turquoise, the glowering purply black mountains of Harris behind, and the deserted island of Taransay (site of the BBC television programme *Castaway 2000*) a mile or so out to sea. You won't find many people here, but the bird life is teeming with long-tailed ducks, eiders and red-breasted mergansers, oystercatchers, northern and red-throated divers. When sun sets behind Taransay, there's no finer place to be.

BEST BEACHES FOR GETTING AWAY FROM IT ALL.

Miranda's favourites...

1 Bryher
2 Barafundle Bay
3 Luskentyre
4 Sandwood Bay
5 Amble Links

Beach Type	Sand
Facilities	Toilet (with disabled facilities)
Activities	Boat trips to nearby Taransay (01859 550260 or www.visit-taransay.com)
Parking	Free car parking
Information	Lochmaddy Tourist Information Centre (01876 500321) or Visit Scotland (0845 2255121)
Lifeguard Cover	None
Dogs	Welcome all year
Useful Websites	www.undiscoveredscotland.co.uk http://perfectday.visitscotland.com www.visithebrides.com

INFORMATION

Beach Type	Sand and pebble
Facilities	None, nearest facilities are in Applecross
Activities	Kayaking courses available (Mountain and Sea Guides: 01502 744394)
Parking	Free parking available
Information	Visit Scotland (0845 2255121)
Lifeguard Cover	None
Dogs	Welcome, but please be responsible
Useful Websites	www.applecross.uk.com
	http://perfectday.visitscotland.com

Applecross

NEAREST TOWN KYLE OF LOCHALSH

You will never forget the hair-raising mountain route to the remote Highland peninsula of Applecross. A steep, single-track road – an old drovers' route to market – twists through acute hairpin bends and 1 in 3 gradients to reach Bealach na Bà, the highest mountain pass in Britain (at 2,044ft/623m). Driving down the mountain towards the coast and Applecross Bay, you catch sight of sparkling aquamarine seas, with the offshore islands of Raasay and Rona, and rugged, purply blue peaks of the Cuillin mountain ridge on Skye behind. It's a wilderness setting of grandeur and glorious beauty, the unspoilt Highland coastline fringed with trees, rivers and open moorland, with red deer, secretive pine martens, otters, hares, and buzzards and the occasional golden eagle.

It is accessed from the village, which is a street of cottages opposite the sea wall with two good eateries – the Applecross Inn and the Potting Shed Restaurant (part of the Applecross House Estate, which manages much of the land on the peninsula). The sheltered bay, on the Inner Sound of Raasay, is almost completely enclosed by the land mass of Skye, and its calm waters are excellent for sea kayaking and other water sports – although don't expect it to be anything other than chilly. The coastline along the peninsula is dotted with small, isolated beaches – Sand, a few miles north of the village, has towering dunes and a wonderful expanse of soft white sand. It's usually quiet, with stunning views to the imposing island peaks just across the Sound.

Calgary Bay
NEAREST TOWN DERVAIG

Mull is Scotland's most dramatic island, with high mountain peaks (including 3,000ft/914m Ben More) and steep cliffs, edged by 300 miles (482km) of rocky coastline, plus the occasional gem of a white sandy beach. Calgary Bay, tucked deep between two craggy headlands in the north-west corner, is the best of them. Its wide, sweeping sands are backed by fertile grassy machair, with wooded slopes beyond. The beach feels secluded and in winter you're likely to be the only person admiring the views to the islands of Tiree and Coll beyond, perhaps catching sight of the golden eagles, rarer white-tailed sea eagles or even otters that have made the island their home. The shallow, aquamarine waters slope gently away and are safe for bathing, and off the rocks you can angle for rock cod, mackerel and sea trout. Basking sharks, dolphins, seals and porpoises are regularly sighted off the coast. There's a steep walk up the northern headland to the ruined village of Inivea (with Highland cattle wandering around), abandoned during the Highland Clearances of the 19th century. There is also a wild camping site at the edge of the beach.

Beach Type	Sand
Facilities	Toilets (with disabled facilities). Caledonian MacBrayne (0870 565000 or www.calmac.co.uk) runs six crossings daily between Oban and Craignure
Activities	No organised activities
Parking	Free parking
Information	Holiday Mull (01689 812377) or Visit Scotland (0845 2255121)
Lifeguard Cover	None
Dogs	Welcome all year
Useful Websites	www.undiscoveredscotland.co.uk http://perfectday.visitscotland.com

Machrihanish Bay
NEAREST TOWN CAMPBELTOWN

You can be forgiven for thinking that Kintyre is an island, so thin is the finger of land that stretches south into the Irish Sea, and so far west of the mainland that the Isle of Arran nestles between the two. Along the western coast of most of Kintyre runs a long shingle beach broken by the occasional rocky outcrop, with dunes and low hills rolling inland dotted with duns (Celtic fortresses). But at Machrihanish Bay there's a 3 mile (5km) curve of sandy beach that is popular among surfers and kite-surfers, who stay at the many local B&Bs or the small camp site nearby. The big evening skies are beautiful here and the sunsets even more dramatic. You can see seals sunning themselves on the rocks and wild goats (pictured right) wandering around the rocky crags on the Gauldrons area of the beach. There's a seabird and wildlife observatory on the western tip.

The surf is best at Westport, an area awarded several prizes for the quality of its sand and water. Nearby is the famous Machrihanish links golf course with its tricky first hole – you have to drive over the beach, which is in play – and views of the islands of Jura and Islay in the far distance. On the inland coast just 5 miles (8km) west is the peninsula's major settlement, Campbeltown, with its whisky distilleries, guesthouses and hotels.

Beach Type	Sand
Facilities	Toilets and a camp site nearby
Activities	Golf available (Machrihanish Golf Club: 01586 810213). This is a popular watersports spot
Parking	Free parking available
Information	Campbeltown Tourist Information Centre (08707 200609) or Visit Scotland (0845 2255121)
Lifeguard Cover	None
Dogs	Welcome all year
Useful Websites	www.kintyre.org http://perfectday.visitscotland.com

UNDERSTANDING WATER QUALITY

To find out the water quality of a beach, the best place to visit is the Good Beach Guide website published by the Marine Conservation Society. They recommend beaches with excellent water quality standards for swimmers who wish to minimise their exposure to water contaminated by sewage. They analyse water sample data from beaches on a yearly basis and grade the results into the following summarised categories:

MCS RECOMMENDED This is the best water quality.
GUIDELINE STANDARD This is good water quality.
BASIC PASS This is the basic legal minimum standard for water quality. There are sewage derived bacteria present in quantities known to cause illness.
FAIL This is poor water quality and has failed the minimum standard. Swimming is not advised in this water.
NOT TESTED No water information is available for this beach. No water sample testing was done in the previous bathing season, and the beach has therefore not been graded by MCS.

To find out further information on the details discussed, visit: www.goodbeachguide.co.uk.

The Marine Conservation Society (MCS) is the UK charity that campaigns for the protection of our seas, shores and marine wildlife. They take action to stop pollution of the sea, run the Adopt-A-Beach campaign that organises thousands of volunteers to help clear litter from our beaches, and use supporters around the coast who gather information on marine animals like basking sharks, turtles and jellyfish. They also tackle the problems of over-fishing and campaign for marine reserves to protect wildlife. If you want to know more about MCS and how you can help them to protect our seas, visit: www.mcsuk.org.

USEFUL WEBSITES

ADOPT A BEACH www.adoptabeach.org.uk

ARCHAEOLOGICAL DIVERS ASSOCIATION
www.underwater-archaeology.org.uk

BEACH HUT RENTAL AND SALES
www.beach-huts.com

BLUE FLAG BEACHES www.blueflag.org

BOTANICAL SOCIETY OF THE BRITISH ISLES
www.bsbi.org.uk

BRITISH BEACH VOLLEYBALL
www.beach-volleyball.co.uk

BRITISH CYCLING www.britishcycling.org.uk

BRITISH DIVERS MARINE LIFE RESCUE
www.bdmlr.org.uk

BRITISH HORSE SOCIETY www.bhs.org.uk

BRITISH NATURISM
www.british-naturism.org.uk/beaches

BRITISH SUB-AQUA CLUB www.bsac.com

BRITISH SURFING ASSOCIATION
www.britsurf.co.uk

BRITISH WATERSKI ONLINE
www.britishwaterski.org.uk

BYWAYS AND BRIDLEWAYS TRUST
www.bbtrust.org.uk

CAMPING AND CARAVANNING CLUB
www.campingandcaravanningclub.co.uk

CANOE AND KAYAK UK
www.canoekayak.co.uk

COAST STEERING
www.whatiscoasteering.co.uk

ENGLAND'S GOLF COAST
www.englandsgolfcoast.com

ENJOY ENGLAND www.enjoyengland.com

MARINE AND COASTGUARD ASSOCIATION
www.mcga.gov.uk

MARINE CONSERVATION SOCIETY
www.mcsuk.org

NATIONAL TRUST (INCLUDING NORTHERN IRELAND
AND WALES) www.nationaltrust.org.uk

NATIONAL TRUST FOR SCOTLAND
www.nts.org.uk

NATIONAL WATER SAFETY FORUM
www.nationalbeachsafety.org.uk

NATURAL ENGLAND
www.naturalengland.org.uk

NORTHERN IRELAND TOURIST BOARD
www.discovernorthernireland.com

RSPB www.rspb.org.uk

ROYAL NATIONAL LIFEBOAT INSTITUTE
www.rnli.org.uk

ROYAL YACHTING ASSOCIATION
www.rya.org.uk

SCOTTISH CAMPING AND CARAVANNING
www.scottishcamping.com

SEABIRD GROUP www.seabirdgroup.org.uk

SEA FISHING
www.sea-fishing.org

SEA KAYAKING www.seakayakinguk.com

SEA SEARCH http://seasearch.wisshost.net

SOUTH WEST COAST PATH
www.southwestcoastpath.com

SURFERS AGAINST SEWAGE
www.sas.org.uk

SUSTRANS (SUSTAINABLE TRANSPORT CHARITY)
www.sustrans.org.uk

UK FOSSIL COLLECTING LOCATIONS
www.ukfossils.co.uk

UK WORLD HERITAGE SITES
www.ukworldheritage.org.uk

VISIT BRITAIN www.visitbritain.com

VISIT SCOTLAND www.visitscotland.com

VISIT WALES www.visitwales.com

WHALE AND DOLPHIN CONSERVATION SOCIETY
www.wdcs.org

WILDFOWL AND WETLAND TRUST
www.wwt.org.uk

WILDLIFE TRUSTS www.wildlifetrusts.org

INDEX

PICTURE CREDITS

First published in the United Kingdom in 2009 by
Pavilion Books
10 Southcombe Street
London, W14 0RA

An imprint of Anova Books Company Ltd

Text copyright © Jane Phillimore and Miranda Krestovnikoff 2009
Design copyright © Anova Books 2009

The moral right of the author has been asserted.

Associate Publisher: Anna Cheifetz
Project Editor: Katie Deane
Editor: Nina Sharman
Proofreader: Sharon Amos
Design and Cover: Georgina Hewitt
Production: Rebekah Cheyne
Layout: Sarah Rock
Maps: David Atkinson, Hand Made Maps Ltd
Index: Michelle Clarke
Picture Research: Emma O'Neill

ISBN 978-1-86205-858-3

A CIP catalogue record for this book is available from the British Library.

10 9 8 7 6 5 4 3 2 1

Reproduction by Mission Productions Ltd, Hong Kong
Printed and bound by 1010 Printing International, China

www.anovabooks.com

Cover image: Getty Images/Ingine
Miranda Krestovnikoff image (cover and interior): courtesy of John Widdup